GRANDMA COOKBOOK

Easy, Timeless, and Heartwarming Recipes Your Family Will Love, Featuring Fresh, Handpicked Ingredients | Includes Tips and Grandma's Time-Honored Cooking Techniques

HELEN BAKER

© Copyright 2024 Helen Baker

All rights reserved.

The content contained within this book may not be reproduced, duplicated or transmitted without direct written permission from the author or the publisher.

Under no circumstances will any blame or legal responsibility be held against the publisher, or author, for any damages, reparation, or monetary loss due to the information contained within this book, either directly or indirectly.

This book is copyright protected. It is only for personal use. You cannot amend, distribute, sell, use, quote or paraphrase any part, or the content within this book, without the consent of the author or publisher.

By reading this document, the reader agrees that under no circumstances is the author responsible for any losses, direct or indirect, that are incurred as a result of the use of the information contained within this document, including, but not limited to, errors, omissions, or inaccuracies.

TABLE OF CONTENTS

Introduction 1

Chapter 1 : Sunrise Delights 2

    Cinnamon Swirl French Toast 3

    Buttermilk Blueberry Pancakes 4

    Old-Fashioned Oatmeal With Honeyed Pecans 5

    Grandma's Sunday Sausage Gravy & Biscuits 6

    Classic Eggs Benedict With Creamy Hollandaise 7

    Country Ham And Cheese Omelet 8

    Crispy Hash Browns 9

    Home Fries 10

    Corned Beef Hash 11

    Fluffy Buttermilk Waffles 12

Chapter 2 : Heartwarming Soups & Stews 13

    Chicken Noodle Soup Like Grandma Made 14

    Hearty Beef And Barley Stew 15

    Old-Country Vegetable Soup 16

    Sunday Supper Split Pea Soup 17

    New England Clam Chowder 18

    Grandma's Tomato Basil With A Twist 19

    Creamy Potato Soup 20

    Chicken And Dumpling Soup 21

    Classic French Onion Soup 22

Chapter 3 : Comforting Casseroles 23

    Cheesy Scalloped Potatoes 24

    Classic Tuna Noodle Casserole 25

    Sunday Chicken Pot Pie 26

    Sweet Corn And Green Bean Bake 27

Shepherd's Pie With Love 28

Broccoli And Rice Casserole With Cheese 29

Cheesy Hashbrown Casserole 30

Turkey Tetrazzini Casserole 31

Baked Macaroni And Cheese... 32

Lasagna Bolognese 33

Chapter 4 : Cherished Main Dishes 34

Meatloaf With Brown Sugar Glaze 35

Country Fried Steak With Gravy 36

Stuffed Bell Peppers Like She Made 37

Baked Ham With Pineapple & Cherries 38

Roast Turkey With Sage Dressing 39

Braised Pork Chops With Apples 41

Classic Beef Brisket.. 42

Fried Chicken 43

Bbq Ribs 44

Grilled Salmon With Dill 45

Shrimp And Grits 46

Roast Lamb With Mint Jelly 47

Corned Beef And Cabbage.. 48

Chapter 5 : Savory Sides 49

Creamy Mashed Potatoes.. 50

Green Beans Almondine.. 51

Caramelized Onion And Bacon Brussels Sprouts 52

Glazed Carrots With Brown Sugar 53

Southern Collard Greens 54

Cheddar And Chive Scones 55

Sautéed Mushrooms 56

Zucchini And Tomato Gratin 57

Roasted Asparagus... 58

Garlic Butter Rice 59

Cauliflower Gratin 60

Chapter 6 : Garden-Fresh Salads 61

Grandma's Potato Salad 62

Sweet And Sour Coleslaw 63

Waldorf Salad As She Loved 64

Spinach Salad With Hot Bacon Dressing 65

Caesar Salad 66

Greek Village Salad 67

Cobb Salad 68

Chapter 7 : Beloved Breads & Rolls 69

Skillet Cornbread 70

Sunday Dinner Rolls 71

Grandma's Garlic Knots 72

Whole Wheat Honey Bread 73

Pumpkin Scones 74

Banana Nut Bread 75

Buttermilk Biscuits 76

Angel Biscuits 77

Chapter 8 : Sweet Treats And Memory Makers 78

Old-Fashioned Apple Pie 79

Cherry Cobbler Like She Made 80

Chocolate Fudge Brownies 81

Classic Carrot Cake With Cream Cheese Frosting 82

Strawberry Rhubarb Crisp 83

Homemade Vanilla Ice Cream 84

Peach Cobbler 85

Blackberry Pie 86

Red Velvet Cake 87

Apple Cider Doughnuts 88

Chapter 9 : Exclusive Bonuses 89

Chapter 10 : Cooking Conversions 90

Conclusion 92

INTRODUCTION

Welcome to my cozy kitchen, dear ones! This cookbook is your gateway to a world filled with the warmth of grandmotherly love and the comforting aroma of home-cooked meals. Each recipe is a cherished heirloom, passed down through generations, ready to nourish both body and soul.

Before we begin, let's equip your kitchen with some essentials. A good set of knives, a sturdy mixer, and a range of mixing bowls are crucial. Don't forget a reliable cast iron skillet, versatile baking dishes, and a collection of pots and pans. With these tools, you'll be ready to tackle any recipe in this book.

As you explore these pages, remember that cooking is a personal journey. Feel free to adapt these recipes to your taste, substitute ingredients, and let your culinary creativity flow. Whether it's a hearty stew or a delicate dessert, let these dishes inspire you to create and share.

Put on your favorite apron, gather your ingredients, and prepare to fill your home with the smells of baking bread and simmering sauces. Invite your loved ones to share in the joy of meals made with love. Here in Grandma's kitchen, every dish is a celebration of life and family. Let's start this delicious adventure together!

Dear Reader,

I am committed to creating high-quality products, aiming primarily to meet your expectations. Your support is crucial for my development. I would sincerely value your feedback on Amazon once you have finished reading; it would be incredibly meaningful to me. Thank you wholeheartedly.

Warmest regards,

Helen Baker

CHAPTER 1

SUNRISE DELIGHTS

Cinnamon Swirl French Toast

Servings: 4

Ingredients:

- 8 slices of cinnamon swirl bread
- 4 large eggs
- 1 cup whole milk
- 2 tsp vanilla extract
- 1/2 tsp ground cinnamon
- 4 tbsp unsalted butter
- Maple syrup, for serving
- Powdered sugar, for dusting
- Fresh berries (optional), for serving

Nutritional Values (per serving):

- Calories: 350
- Fat: 18g
- Saturated Fat: 5g
- Cholesterol: 96mg
- Sodium: 210mg
- Carbohydrates: 34g
- Fiber: 2g
- Sugars: 15g
- Protein: 9g

Instructions:

Begin by whisking together the eggs, milk, vanilla, and a hint of cinnamon in a shallow bowl until the mixture is perfectly smooth. Lovingly soak each slice of the cinnamon swirl bread in the batter, letting them absorb the flavors for 30 seconds on each side. Warm a skillet over medium heat and melt a tablespoon of butter until it sizzles softly. Gently cook each bread slice for 2-3 minutes on each side until they turn a delightful golden brown. Serve your French toast warm, lovingly drizzled with maple syrup and a sprinkle of powdered sugar. If it pleases you, crown them with fresh berries for a splash of color and freshness.

Buttermilk Blueberry Pancakes

Servings: 4

Ingredients:

- 2 cups all-purpose flour
- 2 tablespoons sugar
- 2 teaspoons baking powder
- 1 teaspoon baking soda
- 1/2 teaspoon salt
- 2 cups buttermilk
- 2 large eggs
- 4 tablespoons unsalted butter, melted
- 1 cup blueberries (fresh or frozen)
- Additional butter for greasing the pan
- Maple syrup, for serving

Nutritional Values (per serving):

- Calories: 350
- Fat: 12g
- Saturated Fat: 6g
- Cholesterol: 110mg
- Sodium: 530mg
- Carbohydrates: 50g
- Fiber: 2g
- Sugars: 15g
- Protein: 10g

Instructions:

Begin by whisking together the flour, sugar, baking powder, baking soda, and salt in a large bowl until evenly combined. In a separate bowl, whisk together the buttermilk, eggs, and melted butter until smooth. Gently fold the wet mixture into the dry ingredients. Do not overmix, the batter should remain slightly lumpy. Once combined, gently fold in the blueberries.

Heat a large skillet over medium heat and melt a small pat of butter until it sizzles softly. Pour 1/4 cup of batter for each pancake onto the skillet and cook for 2-3 minutes on each side, or until golden brown and bubbles form on the surface. Flip and cook until the second side is golden.

Serve your pancakes warm, stacked high, and drizzled with maple syrup. Add a few extra blueberries on top for a pop of freshness. Enjoy these delightful, fluffy pancakes with your loved ones as a perfect start to the day!

Old-Fashioned Oatmeal with Honeyed Pecans

Servings: 4

Ingredients:

- 2 cups old-fashioned rolled oats
- 4 cups water
- 1/2 teaspoon salt
- 1/4 cup honey
- 1/2 cup pecans, chopped
- Milk or cream, for serving

Nutritional Values (per serving):

- Calories: 290
- Fat: 10g
- Saturated Fat: 1g
- Cholesterol: 0mg
- Sodium: 300mg
- Carbohydrates: 45g
- Fiber: 5g
- Sugars: 12g
- Protein: 8g

Instructions:

Start by bringing the water and salt to a gentle boil in a medium saucepan. Stir in the oats, reduce the heat to low, and let the oats simmer, stirring occasionally, until they are soft and creamy, about 5 minutes.

While the oatmeal cooks, toast the pecans in a small pan over medium heat until fragrant, about 2-3 minutes. Drizzle honey over the pecans, stirring to coat them evenly, then remove from heat.

Spoon the warm oatmeal into bowls, top with honeyed pecans, and add a splash of milk or cream. The oatmeal can also be served with an extra drizzle of honey or a sprinkle of cinnamon for additional flavor. Serve immediately for a cozy, comforting breakfast that brings warmth and sweetness to your morning.

Grandma's Sunday Sausage Gravy & Biscuits

Servings: 4

Ingredients for Sausage Gravy:

- 1 pound pork sausage
- 1/4 cup all-purpose flour
- 3 cups milk
- Salt and black pepper, to taste

Ingredients for Biscuits:

- 2 cups all-purpose flour
- 1 tablespoon baking powder
- 1/2 teaspoon salt
- 1/2 cup unsalted butter, cold and cubed
- 3/4 cup buttermilk

Nutritional Values (per serving):

- Calories: 580
- Fat: 38g
- Saturated Fat: 15g
- Cholesterol: 110mg
- Sodium: 1240mg
- Carbohydrates: 36g
- Fiber: 1g
- Sugars: 6g
- Protein: 25g

Instructions for Biscuits

Begin by preheating your oven to 425°F. In a large bowl, whisk together the flour, baking powder, and salt. Using a pastry cutter or your hands, cut the cold butter into the dry ingredients until the mixture resembles coarse crumbs. Slowly stir in the buttermilk until the dough comes together, being careful not to overmix.

Turn the dough onto a floured surface, gently pat it down to about 1-inch thickness, and cut out biscuits using a 2-inch round cutter. Place the biscuits on a baking sheet and bake for 12-15 minutes, or until golden brown. Let them cool slightly while you prepare the gravy.

Instructions for Sausage Gravy

Begin by browning the sausage in a large skillet over medium heat, breaking it up as it cooks until fully browned and crumbly. Sprinkle the flour evenly over the sausage and stir to combine. Let the flour cook for 1-2 minutes to eliminate any raw taste.

Gradually pour in the milk, stirring constantly to avoid lumps. Continue cooking and stirring until the gravy thickens, about 5-10 minutes. Season generously with salt and pepper to taste.

Serve the sausage gravy over warm biscuits, splitting the biscuits in half and pouring the rich, creamy gravy over the top. Enjoy this classic comfort food, perfect for a hearty Sunday breakfast with family.

Classic Eggs Benedict With Creamy Hollandaise

Servings: 4

Ingredients:

- 8 eggs
- 4 English muffins, split and toasted
- 8 slices Canadian bacon
- 1 recipe Hollandaise sauce (recipe below)
- Paprika or chopped chives, for garnish

Hollandaise Sauce:

- 3 egg yolks
- 1 tablespoon lemon juice
- 1/2 cup unsalted butter, melted
- Salt, to taste

Nutritional Values (per serving):

- Calories: 450
- Fat: 32g
- Saturated Fat: 16g
- Cholesterol: 475mg
- Sodium: 860mg
- Carbohydrates: 25g
- Fiber: 1g
- Sugars: 2g
- Protein: 20g

Instructions:

Start by preparing the **Hollandaise sauce**. In a heatproof bowl over simmering water, whisk together the egg yolks and lemon juice over low heat until pale and slightly thickened. Slowly drizzle in the melted butter while continuously whisking, creating a creamy, velvety sauce. Remove from heat and season with a pinch of salt. Keep warm.

For the **Eggs Benedict**, heat a skillet over medium heat and cook the Canadian bacon slices until browned on both sides. In the meantime, poach the eggs by simmering water in a pot. Crack each egg into a small dish, gently slip it into the water, and cook until the whites are set but the yolk remains soft, about 3-4 minutes.

To assemble, place a slice of Canadian bacon on each toasted English muffin half, followed by a poached egg. Generously spoon the creamy Hollandaise sauce over the top and garnish with a sprinkle of paprika or chopped chives. Serve immediately for a breakfast that feels like a celebration, full of elegance and comfort.

Country Ham And Cheese Omelet

Servings: 4

Ingredients:

- 8 large eggs
- 1/4 cup whole milk
- 1 cup cooked ham, diced
- 1 cup shredded cheddar cheese
- 2 tablespoons butter
- Salt and black pepper, to taste
- Chopped chives (optional, for garnish)

Nutritional Values (per serving):

- Calories: 320
- Fat: 22g
- Saturated Fat: 10g
- Cholesterol: 375mg
- Sodium: 680mg
- Carbohydrates: 2g
- Fiber: 0g
- Sugars: 1g
- Protein: 26g

Instructions:

Begin by whisking together the eggs, milk, salt, and pepper in a medium bowl until smooth and well-combined. Heat 1 tablespoon of butter in a large non-stick skillet over medium heat. Pour in half of the egg mixture, allowing it to spread evenly across the pan.

As the eggs begin to set, sprinkle half of the diced ham and shredded cheddar cheese evenly over the surface. Once the edges are firm and the cheese starts to melt, fold the omelet in half using a spatula. Cook for another minute, then slide the omelet onto a plate. Repeat with the remaining egg mixture, ham, and cheese.

Garnish with chopped chives if desired. Serve hot and enjoy this hearty, comforting breakfast that's perfect for starting the day with family.

Crispy Hash Browns

Servings: 4

Ingredients:

- 4 medium russet potatoes, peeled and grated
- 1/4 cup finely chopped onion (optional)
- 2 tablespoons olive oil
- 2 tablespoons butter
- Salt and black pepper, to taste
- Ketchup or hot sauce, for serving (optional)

Nutritional Values (per serving):

- Calories: 210
- Fat: 14g
- Saturated Fat: 6g
- Cholesterol: 25mg
- Sodium: 180mg
- Carbohydrates: 20g
- Fiber: 3g
- Sugars: 1g
- Protein: 2g

Instructions:

Begin by rinsing the grated potatoes in cold water to remove excess starch. Drain and thoroughly pat dry with a clean kitchen towel to remove any moisture. Heat 1 tablespoon of olive oil and 1 tablespoon of butter in a large skillet over medium heat.

Toss the grated potatoes with the chopped onion, if using, and season generously with salt and pepper. Spread the potatoes in an even layer in the skillet, pressing them down gently with a spatula. Cook for 4-5 minutes on one side, until golden brown and crispy. Flip the potatoes and cook for another 4-5 minutes on the other side until they are crisp and cooked through.

Serve the crispy hash browns hot, with ketchup or hot sauce if desired. Enjoy this classic breakfast side, perfect for adding some crunch to your morning meal.

Home Fries

Servings: 4

Ingredients:

- 4 medium russet potatoes, diced into 1/2-inch cubes
- 1 small onion, finely chopped
- 1 green bell pepper, diced
- 2 tablespoons olive oil
- 2 tablespoons butter
- Salt and black pepper, to taste
- Paprika, for seasoning (optional)

Nutritional Values (per serving):

- Calories: 220
- Fat: 12g
- Saturated Fat: 5g
- Cholesterol: 20mg
- Sodium: 180mg
- Carbohydrates: 25g
- Fiber: 3g
- Sugars: 2g
- Protein: 3g

Instructions:

Begin by parboiling the diced potatoes in salted water for 5-7 minutes, or until they are just tender but still firm. Drain the potatoes and set them aside. In a large skillet, heat the olive oil and butter over medium heat.

Add the chopped onion and bell pepper to the skillet, cooking until they soften, about 3-4 minutes. Add the parboiled potatoes to the skillet, spreading them in an even layer. Season generously with salt, black pepper, and paprika, if desired.

Cook the potatoes for 4-5 minutes without stirring to allow them to brown and crisp on one side. Gently flip the potatoes and cook for an additional 4-5 minutes, or until golden and crispy all over. Serve hot as a hearty breakfast side, and enjoy the comforting crunch of these delicious home fries.

Corned Beef Hash

Servings: 4

Ingredients:

- 2 cups cooked corned beef, diced
- 4 medium potatoes, peeled and diced
- 1 small onion, finely chopped
- 2 tablespoons olive oil
- 2 tablespoons butter
- Salt and black pepper, to taste
- Eggs (optional, for serving)

Nutritional Values (per serving):

- Calories: 350
- Fat: 22g
- Saturated Fat: 8g
- Cholesterol: 95mg
- Sodium: 680mg
- Carbohydrates: 22g
- Fiber: 3g
- Sugars: 1g
- Protein: 14g

Instructions:

Begin by parboiling the diced potatoes in salted water for 5-7 minutes, until they are tender but still firm. Drain the potatoes and set them aside. In a large skillet, heat the olive oil and butter over medium heat.

Add the chopped onion to the skillet and cook for 2-3 minutes, or until softened. Add the diced corned beef and potatoes to the skillet, stirring to combine. Spread the mixture evenly across the pan and cook for 4-5 minutes without stirring to let the potatoes and corned beef crisp up.

Gently flip the mixture and continue cooking for another 4-5 minutes, allowing the crisp to form. Season with salt and pepper to taste. Serve hot, with eggs on top if desired, for a traditional breakfast that's packed with flavor and warmth.

Fluffy Buttermilk Waffles

Servings: 4

Ingredients:

- 2 cups all-purpose flour
- 2 tablespoons sugar
- 2 teaspoons baking powder
- 1 teaspoon baking soda
- 1/2 teaspoon salt
- 2 large eggs
- 2 cups buttermilk
- 1/4 cup unsalted butter, melted
- 1 teaspoon vanilla extract
- Butter and maple syrup, for serving

Nutritional Values (per serving):

- Calories: 380
- Fat: 18g
- Saturated Fat: 9g
- Cholesterol: 120mg
- Sodium: 610mg
- Carbohydrates: 44g
- Fiber: 1g
- Sugars: 8g
- Protein: 10g

Instructions:

Begin by whisking together the flour, sugar, baking powder, baking soda, and salt in a large bowl. In a separate bowl, whisk together the eggs, buttermilk, melted butter, and vanilla extract until smooth.

Gradually pour the wet ingredients into the dry ingredients, stirring just until combined. Be careful not to overmix—the batter should have some lumps.

Preheat your waffle iron and lightly grease it with butter or non-stick spray. Pour about 1/2 cup of batter into the waffle iron, spreading it evenly. Cook according to your waffle iron's instructions, typically 3-4 minutes, or until golden brown and crisp.

Serve the waffles hot, topped with butter and a drizzle of maple syrup. Enjoy these light, fluffy waffles that are perfect for a comforting breakfast with your family.

CHAPTER 2

HEARTWARMING SOUPS & STEWS

Chicken Noodle Soup Like Grandma Made

Servings: 6

Ingredients:

- 1 whole chicken (about 3-4 lbs), cut into pieces
- 10 cups water
- 2 large carrots, diced
- 2 celery stalks, diced
- 1 onion, chopped
- 3 garlic cloves, minced
- 1 bay leaf
- 1 teaspoon dried thyme
- Salt and pepper, to taste
- 8 oz egg noodles
- Fresh parsley, chopped (optional, for garnish)

Nutritional Values (per serving):

- Calories: 300
- Fat: 10g
- Saturated Fat: 3g
- Cholesterol: 90mg
- Sodium: 450mg
- Carbohydrates: 30g
- Fiber: 3g
- Sugars: 4g
- Protein: 25g

Instructions:

Begin by placing the chicken pieces in a large pot and covering them with water. Bring to a boil, skimming off any foam that rises to the top. Reduce the heat to a simmer, and add the carrots, celery, onion, garlic, bay leaf, and thyme. Season with salt and pepper.

Simmer the soup for about 1 hour, or until the chicken is fully cooked and tender. Remove the chicken from the pot and set it aside to cool slightly. Discard the bay leaf.

Once the chicken is cool enough to handle, remove the meat from the bones and shred it into bite-sized pieces. Return the chicken to the pot, and bring the soup back to a gentle simmer.

Add the egg noodles and cook for an additional 8-10 minutes, or until the noodles are tender. Adjust seasoning with salt and pepper to taste.

Ladle the hot soup into bowls and garnish with fresh parsley if desired. Serve this comforting, homemade chicken noodle soup to warm up the whole family on chilly days.

Hearty Beef And Barley Stew

Servings: 4

Ingredients:

- 1 lb beef stew meat, cut into 1-inch cubes
- 2 tablespoons olive oil
- 1 onion, chopped
- 2 carrots, sliced
- 2 celery stalks, sliced
- 3 garlic cloves, minced
- 6 cups beef broth
- 1/2 cup pearl barley
- 2 bay leaves
- 1 teaspoon dried thyme
- Salt and black pepper, to taste
- Fresh parsley, chopped (optional, for garnish)

Nutritional Values (per serving):

- Calories: 450
- Fat: 18g
- Saturated Fat: 5g
- Cholesterol: 90mg
- Sodium: 800mg
- Carbohydrates: 40g
- Fiber: 8g
- Sugars: 6g
- Protein: 32g

Instructions:

In a large pot or Dutch oven, heat the olive oil over medium-high heat. Brown the beef on all sides, working in batches if necessary. Remove the beef and set aside.

In the same pot, add the onion, carrots, and celery, cooking for 5-7 minutes until softened. Add the minced garlic and cook for another minute until fragrant. Return the beef to the pot and stir in the beef broth, barley, bay leaves, and thyme. Season with salt and black pepper to taste.

Bring the stew to a boil, then reduce the heat to low. Cover and simmer for 1 1/2 to 2 hours, or until the beef is tender and the barley is cooked. Remove the bay leaves before serving.

Ladle the stew into bowls and garnish with fresh parsley if desired. Enjoy this hearty, warming dish, perfect for cold evenings.

Old-Country Vegetable Soup

Servings: 4

Ingredients:

- 1 tablespoon olive oil
- 1 onion, chopped
- 2 garlic cloves, minced
- 3 carrots, sliced
- 2 celery stalks, sliced
- 1 large potato, diced
- 1 zucchini, chopped
- 1 can (14.5 oz) diced tomatoes
- 6 cups vegetable broth
- 1 teaspoon dried oregano
- 1 teaspoon dried basil
- Salt and black pepper, to taste
- Fresh parsley, chopped (optional, for garnish)

Nutritional Values (per serving):

- Calories: 220
- Fat: 6g
- Saturated Fat: 1g
- Cholesterol: 0mg
- Sodium: 600mg
- Carbohydrates: 38g
- Fiber: 7g
- Sugars: 10g
- Protein: 5g

Instructions:

In a large pot, heat the olive oil over medium heat. Add the chopped onion and garlic, cooking for 3-4 minutes until softened and fragrant.

Add the carrots, celery, potato, and zucchini, stirring to combine. Pour in the diced tomatoes (with juice) and vegetable broth. Stir in the oregano and basil, then season with salt and black pepper to taste.

Bring the soup to a boil, then reduce the heat and simmer, covered, for 30-40 minutes, or until the vegetables are tender.

Ladle the soup into bowls and garnish with fresh parsley if desired. This classic vegetable soup is simple, nourishing, and perfect for a light, comforting meal.

Sunday Supper Split Pea Soup

Servings: 4

Ingredients:
- 1 tablespoon olive oil
- 1 onion, chopped
- 2 carrots, sliced
- 2 celery stalks, sliced
- 2 garlic cloves, minced
- 1 1/2 cups dried split peas, rinsed
- 6 cups chicken broth
- 1 bay leaf
- 1 teaspoon dried thyme
- 1/2 teaspoon smoked paprika
- Salt and black pepper, to taste
- 1/2 lb ham, diced (optional)
- Fresh parsley, chopped (optional, for garnish)

Nutritional Values (per serving):
- Calories: 340
- Fat: 9g
- Saturated Fat: 2g
- Cholesterol: 30mg
- Sodium: 900mg
- Carbohydrates: 45g
- Fiber: 16g
- Sugars: 6g
- Protein: 24g

Instructions:

In a large pot, heat the olive oil over medium heat. Add the chopped onion, carrots, celery, and garlic, cooking for 5-7 minutes until softened.

Stir in the split peas, chicken broth, bay leaf, thyme, and smoked paprika. If using ham, add it to the pot as well. Season with salt and black pepper to taste.

Bring the soup to a boil, then reduce the heat to low. Cover and simmer for 1-1 1/2 hours, stirring occasionally, until the peas are soft and the soup is thickened. Remove the bay leaf before serving.

Ladle the soup into bowls and garnish with fresh parsley if desired. This hearty split pea soup is a perfect dish for Sunday supper, bringing warmth and comfort to the table.

New England Clam Chowder

Servings: 4

Ingredients:

- 4 slices bacon, chopped
- 1 small onion, diced
- 2 garlic cloves, minced
- 2 large potatoes, peeled and diced
- 2 cups clam juice
- 1 cup heavy cream
- 2 (6.5 oz) cans chopped clams, with juice
- 1 bay leaf
- 1 teaspoon fresh thyme (or 1/2 teaspoon dried)
- Salt and black pepper, to taste
- Fresh parsley, chopped (optional, for garnish)

Nutritional Values (per serving):

- Calories: 400
- Fat: 24g
- Saturated Fat: 12g
- Cholesterol: 80mg
- Sodium: 900mg
- Carbohydrates: 34g
- Fiber: 4g
- Sugars: 3g
- Protein: 16g

Instructions:

In a large pot, cook the chopped bacon over medium heat until crispy, about 5-7 minutes. Remove the bacon with a slotted spoon and set it aside, leaving the bacon grease in the pot.

Add the diced onion and garlic to the pot, sautéing for 3-4 minutes until softened. Stir in the diced potatoes and cook for another minute. Pour in the clam juice and add the bay leaf and thyme. Bring the mixture to a boil, then reduce the heat to low and simmer for 15-20 minutes, or until the potatoes are tender.

Stir in the clams (with juice) and heavy cream, and season with salt and black pepper to taste. Simmer for an additional 5 minutes, then remove the bay leaf.

Ladle the clam chowder into bowls and garnish with the reserved crispy bacon and fresh parsley, if desired. This rich and creamy New England classic is perfect for cold-weather comfort.

Grandma's Tomato Basil with A Twist

Servings: 4

Ingredients:

- 1 tablespoon olive oil
- 1 small onion, chopped
- 2 garlic cloves, minced
- 2 (14.5 oz) cans diced tomatoes
- 1/4 cup fresh basil, chopped (or 1 teaspoon dried)
- 1 cup vegetable broth
- 1/2 cup heavy cream
- 1/4 cup sun-dried tomatoes, chopped
- 1/2 teaspoon red pepper flakes (optional)
- Salt and black pepper, to taste
- Fresh basil leaves, for garnish

Nutritional Values (per serving):

- Calories: 260
- Fat: 18g
- Saturated Fat: 9g
- Cholesterol: 50mg
- Sodium: 550mg
- Carbohydrates: 23g
- Fiber: 5g
- Sugars: 10g
- Protein: 4g

Instructions:

In a large pot, heat the olive oil over medium heat. Add the chopped onion and garlic, cooking for 5-7 minutes until softened and fragrant.

Stir in the diced tomatoes, fresh basil, and vegetable broth. Bring to a simmer and cook for 10-15 minutes, allowing the flavors to meld. Add the chopped sun-dried tomatoes and red pepper flakes (if using) for a touch of heat.

Remove the pot from heat and use an immersion blender to puree the soup until smooth. Stir in the heavy cream and season with salt and black pepper to taste.

Ladle the soup into bowls and garnish with fresh basil leaves. This creamy tomato basil soup with a twist from sun-dried tomatoes brings warmth and a burst of flavor to your table.

Creamy Potato Soup

Servings: 4

Ingredients:

- 4 large russet potatoes, peeled and diced
- 1 small onion, chopped
- 2 garlic cloves, minced
- 4 cups chicken broth
- 1 cup heavy cream
- 1/2 cup sour cream
- 4 slices bacon, cooked and crumbled
- 1/2 cup shredded cheddar cheese
- 2 tablespoons butter
- Salt and black pepper, to taste
- Fresh chives, chopped (optional, for garnish)

Nutritional Values (per serving):

- Calories: 450
- Fat: 28g
- Saturated Fat: 14g
- Cholesterol: 85mg
- Sodium: 750mg
- Carbohydrates: 40g
- Fiber: 4g
- Sugars: 4g
- Protein: 10g

Instructions:

In a large pot, melt the butter over medium heat. Add the chopped onion and garlic, cooking for 5-7 minutes until softened.

Stir in the diced potatoes and chicken broth. Bring the mixture to a boil, then reduce the heat to low. Cover and simmer for 20-25 minutes, or until the potatoes are tender.

Use an immersion blender to puree the soup until smooth, or leave some chunks for texture. Stir in the heavy cream and sour cream, then season with salt and black pepper to taste.

Ladle the soup into bowls and top with crumbled bacon, shredded cheddar cheese, and fresh chives. This comforting potato soup is rich, creamy, and perfect for a cozy meal.

Chicken And Dumpling Soup

Servings: 4

Ingredients for the Soup:
- 1 tablespoon olive oil
- 1 small onion, chopped
- 2 carrots, sliced
- 2 celery stalks, sliced
- 2 garlic cloves, minced
- 6 cups chicken broth
- 1 lb cooked chicken, shredded
- 1 bay leaf
- Salt and black pepper, to taste
- Fresh parsley, chopped (optional, for garnish)

Ingredients for Dumplings:
- 1 cup all-purpose flour
- 1 teaspoon baking powder
- 1/4 teaspoon salt
- 1/2 cup buttermilk
- 2 tablespoons unsalted butter, melted

Nutritional Values (per serving):
- Calories: 400
- Fat: 15g
- Saturated Fat: 6g
- Cholesterol: 95mg
- Sodium: 850mg
- Carbohydrates: 34g
- Fiber: 4g
- Sugars: 5g
- Protein: 28g

Instructions:

In a large pot, heat the olive oil over medium heat. Add the chopped onion, carrots, celery, and garlic, cooking for 5-7 minutes until softened. Stir in the chicken broth, shredded chicken, and bay leaf. Season with salt and black pepper.

Bring the soup to a simmer and cook for 15-20 minutes.

Meanwhile, prepare the dumplings. In a medium bowl, whisk together the flour, baking powder, and salt. Stir in the buttermilk and melted butter until a thick batter forms.

Drop spoonfuls of the dumpling batter into the simmering soup. Cover the pot and cook for 10-12 minutes, or until the dumplings are fluffy and cooked through.

Ladle the soup into bowls and garnish with fresh parsley if desired. This comforting chicken and dumpling soup is a hearty, satisfying dish perfect for family dinners.

Classic French Onion Soup

Servings: 4

Ingredients:

- 4 large onions, thinly sliced
- 3 tablespoons unsalted butter
- 1 tablespoon olive oil
- 1 teaspoon sugar
- 2 garlic cloves, minced
- 6 cups beef broth
- 1/4 cup dry white wine (optional)
- 1 bay leaf
- 1 teaspoon fresh thyme (or 1/2 teaspoon dried)
- Salt and black pepper, to taste
- 4 slices of French bread, toasted
- 1 cup shredded Gruyère or Swiss cheese

Nutritional Values (per serving):

- Calories: 380
- Fat: 22g
- Saturated Fat: 12g
- Cholesterol: 60mg
- Sodium: 900mg
- Carbohydrates: 32g
- Fiber: 4g
- Sugars: 10g
- Protein: 16g

Instructions:

In a large pot, melt the butter with the olive oil over medium heat. Add the sliced onions and sugar, stirring to coat the onions in the butter. Cook for 25-30 minutes, stirring frequently, until the onions are deeply caramelized.

Stir in the garlic and cook for another minute until fragrant. Add the beef broth, white wine (if using), bay leaf, and thyme. Bring the soup to a simmer and cook for 20-25 minutes. Season with salt and black pepper to taste.

Preheat your broiler. Ladle the soup into oven-safe bowls, top each bowl with a slice of toasted French bread, and sprinkle generously with shredded Gruyère cheese.

Place the bowls under the broiler for 2-3 minutes, or until the cheese is melted and bubbly. Serve immediately and enjoy this rich, savory French onion soup that's a true classic.

CHAPTER 3

COMFORTING CASSEROLES

Cheesy Scalloped Potatoes

Servings: 4

Ingredients:

- 4 large russet potatoes, thinly sliced
- 1 small onion, thinly sliced
- 2 tablespoons unsalted butter
- 2 tablespoons all-purpose flour
- 1 1/2 cups whole milk
- 1 cup shredded cheddar cheese
- 1/2 cup shredded mozzarella cheese
- 1/4 teaspoon garlic powder
- Salt and black pepper, to taste
- Fresh parsley, chopped (optional, for garnish)

Nutritional Values (per serving):

- Calories: 380
- Fat: 18g
- Saturated Fat: 11g
- Cholesterol: 50mg
- Sodium: 450mg
- Carbohydrates: 45g
- Fiber: 4g
- Sugars: 6g
- Protein: 12g

Instructions:

Preheat your oven to 375°F. Grease a 9x9-inch baking dish and set aside.

In a medium saucepan, melt the butter over medium heat. Stir in the flour and cook for 1-2 minutes to form a roux. Gradually whisk in the milk, stirring constantly until the mixture thickens, about 3-4 minutes. Remove from heat and stir in the garlic powder, shredded cheddar, and mozzarella cheeses. Season with salt and black pepper to taste.

Layer half of the thinly sliced potatoes in the prepared baking dish, then top with half of the sliced onions. Pour half of the cheese sauce over the potato and onion layer. Repeat the layers with the remaining potatoes, onions, and cheese sauce.

Cover the dish with foil and bake for 45 minutes. Remove the foil and bake for an additional 15 minutes, or until the potatoes are tender and the top is golden and bubbly.

Let the scalloped potatoes rest for a few minutes before serving. Garnish with fresh parsley if desired. These creamy, cheesy potatoes make the perfect side dish for any meal.

Classic Tuna Noodle Casserole

Servings: 6

Ingredients:

- 12 oz egg noodles
- 2 cans (5 oz each) tuna, drained and flaked
- 1 can (10.5 oz) cream of mushroom soup
- 1 cup milk
- 1 cup frozen peas
- 1 cup shredded cheddar cheese
- 1/2 cup breadcrumbs
- 2 tablespoons butter, melted
- Salt and black pepper, to taste

Nutritional Values (per serving):

- Calories: 420
- Fat: 18g
- Saturated Fat: 8g
- Cholesterol: 75mg
- Sodium: 720mg
- Carbohydrates: 45g
- Fiber: 3g
- Sugars: 4g
- Protein: 22g

Instructions:

Begin by preheating your oven to 375°F. Cook the egg noodles according to the package directions, then drain and set aside.

In a large mixing bowl, combine the cream of mushroom soup and milk until smooth. Stir in the drained tuna, frozen peas, and half of the shredded cheese. Season with salt and pepper to taste.

Fold the cooked noodles into the mixture until evenly coated. Pour the tuna mixture into a greased 9x13-inch baking dish. Sprinkle the remaining cheese over the top.

In a small bowl, combine the breadcrumbs and melted butter. Sprinkle the breadcrumb mixture evenly over the casserole.

Bake for 25-30 minutes, or until the casserole is bubbly and the top is golden brown. Serve warm, and enjoy this classic comfort dish that brings back memories of grandma's kitchen.

Sunday Chicken Pot Pie

Servings: 6

Ingredients:

- 1 lb cooked chicken, shredded
- 1 cup carrots, diced
- 1 cup peas (frozen or fresh)
- 1/2 cup celery, diced
- 1/2 cup onion, chopped
- 1/4 cup unsalted butter
- 1/4 cup all-purpose flour
- 2 cups chicken broth
- 1 cup whole milk
- Salt and black pepper, to taste
- 1 sheet refrigerated pie crust (or homemade)

Nutritional Values (per serving):

- Calories: 480
- Fat: 28g
- Saturated Fat: 12g
- Cholesterol: 90mg
- Sodium: 670mg
- Carbohydrates: 35g
- Fiber: 4g
- Sugars: 3g
- Protein: 22g

Instructions:

Begin by preheating your oven to 400°F. In a large skillet, melt the butter over medium heat. Add the onion, celery, and carrots, and sauté for 5-7 minutes, until the vegetables are softened.

Stir in the flour and cook for 1-2 minutes to eliminate the raw taste. Gradually whisk in the chicken broth and milk, stirring constantly until the sauce thickens, about 3-5 minutes. Season with salt and pepper to taste.

Stir in the shredded chicken and peas, mixing until evenly combined. Pour the filling into a greased 9-inch pie dish.

Roll out the pie crust and place it over the top of the filling, pressing the edges to seal. Cut a few small slits in the top to allow steam to escape.

Bake for 30-35 minutes, or until the crust is golden brown and the filling is bubbling. Let the pot pie cool slightly before serving. Enjoy this cozy, heartwarming dish, perfect for Sunday family dinners.

Sweet Corn And Green Bean Bake

Servings: 6

Ingredients:

- 2 cups fresh or frozen green beans, trimmed
- 1 can (15 oz) sweet corn, drained
- 1/2 cup sour cream
- 1/2 cup shredded cheddar cheese
- 1/2 cup crushed crackers or breadcrumbs
- 2 tablespoons unsalted butter, melted
- Salt and black pepper, to taste

Nutritional Values (per serving):

- Calories: 220
- Fat: 14g
- Saturated Fat: 7g
- Cholesterol: 35mg
- Sodium: 290mg
- Carbohydrates: 18g
- Fiber: 2g
- Sugars: 4g
- Protein: 5g

Instructions:

Begin by preheating your oven to 350°F. If using fresh green beans, blanch them in salted boiling water for 3-4 minutes until tender but still crisp. Drain and set aside.

In a large mixing bowl, combine the green beans, drained corn, sour cream, and half of the shredded cheddar cheese. Season with salt and pepper to taste, and stir until everything is evenly coated.

Pour the mixture into a greased 9x9-inch baking dish. Sprinkle the remaining cheese on top.

In a small bowl, mix the crushed crackers or breadcrumbs with the melted butter. Evenly sprinkle the buttered crumbs over the top of the casserole.

Bake for 25-30 minutes, or until the casserole is hot and bubbling, and the top is golden brown. Serve this comforting side dish warm, perfect for family gatherings and holiday dinners.

Shepherd's Pie with Love

Servings: 6

Ingredients:
- 1 lb ground beef or lamb
- 1 onion, finely chopped
- 1 carrot, diced
- 1 cup frozen peas
- 2 tablespoons all-purpose flour
- 1 cup beef broth
- 1 tablespoon tomato paste
- 4 cups mashed potatoes (prepared from scratch or leftover)
- 2 tablespoons butter, melted
- Salt and black pepper, to taste

Nutritional Values (per serving):
- Calories: 450
- Fat: 23g
- Saturated Fat: 11g
- Cholesterol: 85mg
- Sodium: 500mg
- Carbohydrates: 40g
- Fiber: 5g
- Sugars: 4g
- Protein: 20g

Instructions:

Begin by preheating your oven to 400°F. In a large skillet, cook the ground beef (or lamb) over medium heat until browned, breaking it up with a spoon as it cooks. Drain any excess fat, then add the chopped onion and carrot. Cook for an additional 5-7 minutes, until the vegetables are tender.

Sprinkle the flour over the meat and vegetable mixture, stirring to coat. Stir in the beef broth and tomato paste, cooking for 3-4 minutes until the sauce thickens. Stir in the frozen peas and season with salt and pepper to taste.

Transfer the meat mixture to a greased 9x9-inch baking dish. Spread the mashed potatoes evenly over the top, making sure to cover the filling completely. Brush the melted butter over the mashed potatoes for a golden finish.

Bake for 20-25 minutes, or until the top is golden and the filling is bubbling around the edges. Let the shepherd's pie cool for a few minutes before serving. Enjoy this classic, comforting dish that brings warmth and love to your table.

Broccoli And Rice Casserole With Cheese

Servings: 6

Ingredients:

- 4 cups broccoli florets (fresh or frozen)
- 2 cups cooked white rice
- 1 cup shredded cheddar cheese
- 1 can (10.5 oz) cream of mushroom soup
- 1/2 cup milk
- 1/2 cup crushed crackers or breadcrumbs
- 2 tablespoons butter, melted
- Salt and black pepper, to taste

Nutritional Values (per serving):

- Calories: 320
- Fat: 15g
- Saturated Fat: 8g
- Cholesterol: 45mg
- Sodium: 600mg
- Carbohydrates: 36g
- Fiber: 3g
- Sugars: 3g
- Protein: 12g

Instructions:

Begin by preheating your oven to 350°F. Steam or blanch the broccoli florets for 3-4 minutes, until they are bright green and tender but still crisp. Drain and set aside.

In a large mixing bowl, combine the cooked rice, shredded cheddar cheese, cream of mushroom soup, and milk. Stir in the broccoli florets, and season with salt and pepper to taste.

Pour the mixture into a greased 9x9-inch baking dish. In a small bowl, mix the crushed crackers or breadcrumbs with the melted butter, then sprinkle the mixture over the top of the casserole.

Bake for 25-30 minutes, or until the casserole is hot and bubbly, and the topping is golden brown. Serve warm as a comforting side dish or a light meal on its own.

Cheesy Hashbrown Casserole

Servings: 6

Ingredients:

- 1 (30 oz) bag frozen hash browns, thawed
- 1 can (10.5 oz) cream of chicken soup
- 1 cup sour cream
- 1/2 cup melted butter
- 1 1/2 cups shredded cheddar cheese
- 1/2 cup chopped onion
- 1 cup crushed cornflakes or breadcrumbs
- 2 tablespoons butter, melted (for topping)
- Salt and black pepper, to taste

Nutritional Values (per serving):

- Calories: 450
- Fat: 28g
- Saturated Fat: 14g
- Cholesterol: 60mg
- Sodium: 650mg
- Carbohydrates: 40g
- Fiber: 2g
- Sugars: 2g
- Protein: 10g

Instructions:

Begin by preheating your oven to 350°F. In a large mixing bowl, combine the thawed hash browns, cream of chicken soup, sour cream, melted butter, shredded cheddar cheese, and chopped onion. Stir until well-mixed, then season with salt and pepper to taste.

Pour the mixture into a greased 9x13-inch baking dish and spread it evenly. In a small bowl, mix the crushed cornflakes or breadcrumbs with the melted butter, then sprinkle the mixture over the top of the casserole.

Bake for 45-50 minutes, or until the casserole is golden brown and bubbly around the edges. Serve warm and enjoy this comforting, cheesy dish that's perfect for breakfast, brunch, or as a side to a family meal.

Turkey Tetrazzini Casserole

Servings: 6

Ingredients:

- 3 cups cooked turkey, shredded or cubed
- 12 oz spaghetti, cooked and drained
- 1 cup mushrooms, sliced
- 1 small onion, chopped
- 2 tablespoons butter
- 1 can (10.5 oz) cream of mushroom soup
- 1 cup chicken broth
- 1/2 cup sour cream
- 1 cup shredded Parmesan cheese
- 1/2 cup breadcrumbs
- Salt and black pepper, to taste

Nutritional Values (per serving):

- Calories: 550
- Fat: 22g
- Saturated Fat: 10g
- Cholesterol: 80mg
- Sodium: 800mg
- Carbohydrates: 58g
- Fiber: 3g
- Sugars: 4g
- Protein: 34g

Instructions:

Begin by preheating your oven to 350°F. In a large skillet, melt the butter over medium heat. Add the chopped onion and mushrooms, and sauté for 5-7 minutes, until softened and slightly golden.

In a large bowl, combine the cream of mushroom soup, chicken broth, and sour cream, mixing until smooth. Stir in the cooked turkey, sautéed vegetables, and cooked spaghetti. Season with salt and black pepper to taste.

Transfer the mixture to a greased 9x13-inch baking dish. Sprinkle the top with shredded Parmesan cheese and breadcrumbs.

Bake for 25-30 minutes, or until the casserole is bubbly and golden on top. Serve this cozy, creamy dish as a perfect way to use leftover turkey and bring warmth to any family dinner.

Baked Macaroni And Cheese

Servings: 6

Ingredients:

- 12 oz elbow macaroni
- 2 cups shredded cheddar cheese
- 1/2 cup shredded mozzarella cheese
- 3 tablespoons unsalted butter
- 3 tablespoons all-purpose flour
- 2 cups whole milk
- 1/2 teaspoon mustard powder (optional)
- 1/2 cup breadcrumbs
- 1 tablespoon butter, melted (for topping)
- Salt and black pepper, to taste

Nutritional Values (per serving):

- Calories: 520
- Fat: 27g
- Saturated Fat: 15g
- Cholesterol: 75mg
- Sodium: 550mg
- Carbohydrates: 50g
- Fiber: 2g
- Sugars: 5g
- Protein: 20g

Instructions:

Begin by preheating your oven to 350°F. Cook the elbow macaroni according to the package instructions until al dente. Drain and set aside.

In a large saucepan, melt the butter over medium heat. Stir in the flour and cook for 1-2 minutes to form a roux. Slowly whisk in the milk, stirring constantly to avoid lumps. Cook until the sauce thickens, about 3-5 minutes. Stir in the mustard powder (if using), and season with salt and pepper to taste.

Remove the sauce from heat and stir in the shredded cheddar and mozzarella cheeses, mixing until the cheese is fully melted and smooth. Add the cooked macaroni to the cheese sauce, stirring until evenly coated.

Pour the macaroni and cheese into a greased 9x13-inch baking dish. In a small bowl, combine the breadcrumbs and melted butter, then sprinkle the mixture over the top.

Bake for 25-30 minutes, or until the top is golden brown and the cheese is bubbling. Serve warm and enjoy this comforting, cheesy dish perfect for family dinners.

Lasagna Bolognese

Servings: 8

Ingredients:

- 12 lasagna noodles
- 1 lb ground beef
- 1/2 lb ground pork
- 1 small onion, chopped
- 2 garlic cloves, minced
- 1 can (28 oz) crushed tomatoes
- 2 tablespoons tomato paste
- 1 teaspoon dried oregano
- 1 teaspoon dried basil
- 2 cups ricotta cheese
- 1 egg
- 2 cups shredded mozzarella cheese
- 1/2 cup grated Parmesan cheese
- Salt and black pepper, to taste

Nutritional Values (per serving):

- Calories: 620
- Fat: 30g
- Saturated Fat: 14g
- Cholesterol: 110mg
- Sodium: 850mg
- Carbohydrates: 45g
- Fiber: 4g
- Sugars: 8g
- Protein: 38g

Instructions:

Begin by preheating your oven to 375°F. Cook the lasagna noodles according to the package instructions. Drain and set aside.

In a large skillet, cook the ground beef, pork, onion, and garlic over medium heat until browned. Drain any excess fat and return to heat. Stir in the crushed tomatoes, tomato paste, oregano, basil, and season with salt and pepper to taste. Simmer the sauce for 20 minutes.

In a medium bowl, mix the ricotta cheese with the egg until smooth. Set aside.

To assemble the lasagna, spread a thin layer of the meat sauce on the bottom of a greased 9x13-inch baking dish. Layer 3-4 noodles on top, followed by a layer of ricotta mixture, a layer of meat sauce, and a sprinkle of shredded mozzarella and Parmesan cheeses. Repeat the layers, finishing with a layer of meat sauce and mozzarella cheese on top.

Cover the lasagna with foil and bake for 25 minutes. Remove the foil and bake for an additional 10-15 minutes, or until the cheese is golden and bubbly. Let the lasagna rest for 10 minutes before serving. Enjoy this rich, hearty dish with family and friends.

CHAPTER 4

CHERISHED MAIN DISHES

Meatloaf With Brown Sugar Glaze

Servings: 6

Ingredients:
- 1 1/2 lbs ground beef
- 1/2 cup bread crumbs
- 1/2 cup milk
- 1 egg
- 1 small onion, finely chopped
- 2 tablespoons ketchup
- 1 tablespoon Worcestershire sauce
- Salt and black pepper, to taste

For the Glaze:
- 1/4 cup brown sugar
- 2 tablespoons ketchup
- 1 tablespoon mustard

Nutritional Values (per serving):
- Calories: 420
- Fat: 22g
- Saturated Fat: 9g
- Cholesterol: 130mg
- Sodium: 550mg
- Carbohydrates: 20g
- Fiber: 1g
- Sugars: 12g
- Protein: 35g

Instructions:

Begin by preheating your oven to 350°F. In a large mixing bowl, combine the ground beef, bread crumbs, milk, egg, chopped onion, ketchup, Worcestershire sauce, and season with salt and pepper. Mix until everything is well-combined, but be careful not to overmix.

Shape the mixture into a loaf and place it in a greased loaf pan. In a small bowl, mix together the brown sugar, ketchup, and mustard to create the glaze. Spread the glaze evenly over the top of the meatloaf.

Bake the meatloaf for 55-60 minutes, or until the internal temperature reaches 160°F. Let the meatloaf rest for 10 minutes before slicing. Serve warm and enjoy this classic comfort food with your family.

Country Fried Steak With Gravy

Servings: 4

Ingredients:
- 4 cube steaks (about 1 1/2 lbs total)
- 1 cup all-purpose flour
- 1 teaspoon paprika
- 1/2 teaspoon garlic powder
- 1/2 teaspoon onion powder
- 2 eggs
- 1/4 cup milk
- Salt and black pepper, to taste
- 1/4 cup vegetable oil (for frying)

For the Gravy:
- 2 tablespoons all-purpose flour
- 2 cups milk
- Salt and black pepper, to taste

Nutritional Values (per serving):
- Calories: 520
- Fat: 30g
- Saturated Fat: 9g
- Cholesterol: 220mg
- Sodium: 620mg
- Carbohydrates: 35g
- Fiber: 1g
- Sugars: 5g
- Protein: 28g

Instructions:

Begin by preheating your oven to 200°F to keep the steaks warm while you prepare the gravy. In a shallow bowl, combine the flour, paprika, garlic powder, onion powder, salt, and pepper. In a separate bowl, whisk together the eggs and milk.

Dredge each cube steak in the flour mixture, shaking off the excess. Dip the steak in the egg mixture, then coat it again in the flour mixture, pressing the flour onto the steak.

In a large skillet, heat the vegetable oil over medium heat. Fry the steaks, two at a time, for 3-4 minutes per side, or until golden brown and crispy. Transfer the cooked steaks to a paper towel-lined plate and keep warm in the oven.

To make the gravy, drain most of the oil from the skillet, leaving about 2 tablespoons. Stir in the flour and cook for 1-2 minutes to form a roux. Gradually whisk in the milk, stirring constantly to avoid lumps. Cook the gravy for 3-5 minutes, until thickened. Season with salt and pepper to taste.

Serve the country fried steak with the warm gravy poured over the top. Enjoy this southern classic for a hearty and satisfying meal.

Stuffed Bell Peppers Like She Made

Servings: 6

Ingredients:

- 6 large bell peppers (any color)
- 1 lb ground beef
- 1 cup cooked white rice
- 1 small onion, chopped
- 2 garlic cloves, minced
- 1 can (14.5 oz) diced tomatoes, drained
- 1 teaspoon dried oregano
- 1 teaspoon dried basil
- 1 cup shredded mozzarella cheese
- Salt and black pepper, to taste
- 1/4 cup grated Parmesan cheese

Nutritional Values (per serving):

- Calories: 350
- Fat: 18g
- Saturated Fat: 8g
- Cholesterol: 70mg
- Sodium: 600mg
- Carbohydrates: 28g
- Fiber: 5g
- Sugars: 7g
- Protein: 25g

Instructions:

Begin by preheating your oven to 375°F. Cut the tops off the bell peppers and remove the seeds and membranes. Place the peppers in a large pot of boiling water for 5 minutes to soften. Drain and set them aside.

In a large skillet, cook the ground beef over medium heat until browned. Drain any excess fat, then add the chopped onion and garlic, cooking for another 3-4 minutes until softened. Stir in the diced tomatoes, cooked rice, oregano, basil, salt, and pepper. Simmer for 5 minutes, allowing the flavors to combine.

Remove the skillet from heat and stir in 1/2 cup of the shredded mozzarella cheese.

Stuff each bell pepper with the beef and rice mixture, packing it in tightly. Place the stuffed peppers upright in a greased 9x13-inch baking dish. Sprinkle the remaining mozzarella cheese and Parmesan cheese on top of each pepper.

Cover the dish with foil and bake for 25 minutes. Remove the foil and bake for an additional 10-15 minutes, or until the cheese is golden and bubbly. Serve these hearty, comforting stuffed peppers warm and enjoy the flavors of a true family classic.

Baked Ham With Pineapple & Cherries

Servings: 8

Ingredients:

- 1 (8-10 lb) fully cooked bone-in ham
- 1/2 cup brown sugar
- 1/4 cup honey
- 1 tablespoon Dijon mustard
- 1 can (20 oz) pineapple rings, drained (reserve juice)
- Maraschino cherries
- Toothpicks (for securing pineapple and cherries)

Nutritional Values (per serving):

- Calories: 320
- Fat: 14g
- Saturated Fat: 5g
- Cholesterol: 95mg
- Sodium: 1,100mg
- Carbohydrates: 18g
- Fiber: 1g
- Sugars: 16g
- Protein: 34g

Instructions:

Begin by preheating your oven to 325°F. Place the ham in a large roasting pan, flat side down. In a small bowl, mix together the brown sugar, honey, mustard, and 2 tablespoons of the reserved pineapple juice to create the glaze.

Score the surface of the ham in a diamond pattern using a sharp knife, then brush the glaze generously over the ham. Arrange the pineapple rings on the ham, securing each one with a toothpick. Place a cherry in the center of each pineapple ring and secure it with a toothpick.

Cover the ham loosely with foil and bake for 1 1/2 to 2 hours, basting with the glaze every 30 minutes. For the last 30 minutes, remove the foil to allow the ham to brown.

Let the ham rest for 10 minutes before slicing. Serve this sweet and savory dish warm, perfect for holiday gatherings or special family meals.

Roast Turkey With Sage Dressing

Servings: 8-10

Ingredients for Turkey:
- 1 (12-14 lb) whole turkey, thawed
- 1/4 cup olive oil or melted butter
- 2 teaspoons salt
- 1 teaspoon black pepper
- 1 teaspoon dried sage
- 1 teaspoon garlic powder

Ingredients for Sage Dressing:
- 8 cups cubed bread (day-old works best)
- 1/2 cup butter
- 1 onion, chopped
- 2 celery stalks, chopped
- 1 teaspoon dried sage
- 1 teaspoon dried thyme
- 1/2 teaspoon salt
- 1/2 teaspoon black pepper
- 2-3 cups chicken or turkey broth

Nutritional Values (per serving):
- Calories: 450
- Fat: 22g
- Saturated Fat: 8g
- Cholesterol: 140mg
- Sodium: 900mg
- Carbohydrates: 26g
- Fiber: 2g
- Sugars: 3g
- Protein: 38g

Instructions:

For the Turkey:

Begin by preheating your oven to 325°F. Rinse the turkey inside and out, then pat it dry with paper towels. Rub the olive oil or melted butter all over the turkey, and season generously with salt, pepper, sage, and garlic powder.

Place the turkey on a rack in a roasting pan, breast side up. Tuck the wings under the body and tie the legs together with kitchen twine. Roast the turkey for 3 to 3 1/2 hours, or until a meat thermometer inserted into the thickest part of the thigh reads 165°F. Baste the turkey with the pan drippings every 30-40 minutes to keep it moist.

Once done, let the turkey rest for 20 minutes before carving.

For the Sage Dressing:

While the turkey is roasting, prepare the dressing. In a large skillet, melt the butter over medium heat. Add the chopped onion and celery, cooking until softened, about 5-7 minutes. Stir in the sage, thyme, salt, and pepper.

In a large mixing bowl, combine the cubed bread and the sautéed onion and celery mixture. Gradually add 2 cups of broth, stirring until the bread is moistened but not soggy. Add more broth as needed.

Transfer the dressing to a greased 9x13-inch baking dish. Cover with foil and bake at 350°F for 25-30 minutes, then remove the foil and bake for an additional 10 minutes to crisp the top.

Serve the roasted turkey alongside the sage dressing for a traditional and flavorful holiday meal that will bring everyone to the table with joy.

Braised Pork Chops With Apples

Servings: 4

Ingredients:

- 4 bone-in pork chops (about 1-inch thick)
- 2 tablespoons olive oil
- 2 apples, cored and sliced
- 1 large onion, thinly sliced
- 1/2 cup apple cider
- 1/2 cup chicken broth
- 1 tablespoon Dijon mustard
- 1 tablespoon fresh thyme (or 1 teaspoon dried)
- Salt and black pepper, to taste

Nutritional Values (per serving):

- Calories: 450
- Fat: 24g
- Saturated Fat: 8g
- Cholesterol: 100mg
- Sodium: 500mg
- Carbohydrates: 20g
- Fiber: 3g
- Sugars: 12g
- Protein: 38g

Instructions:

Begin by seasoning both sides of the pork chops with salt and pepper. In a large skillet, heat the olive oil over medium-high heat. Sear the pork chops for 2-3 minutes per side, until they are nicely browned. Remove the pork chops from the skillet and set aside.

In the same skillet, add the sliced apples and onion. Cook for 4-5 minutes, stirring occasionally, until the onions are soft and the apples are lightly browned.

Add the apple cider, chicken broth, Dijon mustard, and thyme to the skillet. Stir to combine, scraping up any browned bits from the bottom of the pan. Bring the mixture to a simmer.

Return the pork chops to the skillet, nestling them into the apple and onion mixture. Cover the skillet and reduce the heat to low. Simmer for 25-30 minutes, or until the pork chops are tender and cooked through.

Serve the braised pork chops with the apples and onions spooned over the top. Enjoy this cozy, comforting dish that brings together sweet and savory flavors in a perfect balance.

Classic Beef Brisket

Servings: 6-8

Ingredients:

- 3-4 lbs beef brisket, trimmed
- 2 tablespoons olive oil
- 1 large onion, sliced
- 4 garlic cloves, minced
- 1 cup beef broth
- 1/2 cup red wine (optional)
- 1 can (14.5 oz) diced tomatoes
- 2 tablespoons tomato paste
- 2 tablespoons Worcestershire sauce
- 1 teaspoon smoked paprika
- Salt and black pepper, to taste

Nutritional Values (per serving):

- Calories: 480
- Fat: 30g
- Saturated Fat: 12g
- Cholesterol: 120mg
- Sodium: 680mg
- Carbohydrates: 10g
- Fiber: 2g
- Sugars: 4g
- Protein: 38g

Instructions:

Preheat your oven to 325°F. Season the brisket generously with salt, pepper, and smoked paprika. In a large Dutch oven or oven-safe pot, heat the olive oil over medium-high heat. Sear the brisket on all sides until browned, about 4-5 minutes per side. Remove the brisket and set aside.

In the same pot, add the sliced onion and cook for 3-4 minutes, until softened. Add the minced garlic and cook for another minute. Stir in the beef broth, red wine (if using), diced tomatoes, tomato paste, and Worcestershire sauce. Bring the mixture to a simmer, scraping up any browned bits from the bottom of the pot.

Return the brisket to the pot, fat side up, nestling it into the sauce. Cover the pot with a tight-fitting lid or foil and transfer it to the oven. Check the meat after 3 hours for tenderness, and braise longer if necessary.

Once done, remove the brisket from the pot and let it rest for 10-15 minutes before slicing against the grain. Serve the brisket with the rich sauce spooned over the top. This slow-cooked, flavorful dish is a true comfort classic, perfect for family dinners and gatherings.

Fried Chicken

Servings: 6

Ingredients:

- 1 whole chicken, cut into pieces
- 2 cups buttermilk
- 2 cups all-purpose flour
- 1 teaspoon paprika
- 1 teaspoon garlic powder
- 1/2 teaspoon cayenne pepper (optional)
- Salt and black pepper, to taste
- Vegetable oil, for frying

Nutritional Values (per serving):

- Calories: 540
- Fat: 30g
- Saturated Fat: 8g
- Cholesterol: 135mg
- Sodium: 560mg
- Carbohydrates: 28g
- Fiber: 2g
- Sugars: 4g
- Protein: 40g

Instructions:

Begin by placing the chicken pieces in a large bowl and covering them with buttermilk. Refrigerate for at least 2 hours, or overnight, to tenderize the chicken.

In a large shallow dish, whisk together the flour, paprika, garlic powder, cayenne pepper (if using), salt, and black pepper. Remove the chicken from the buttermilk, letting the excess drip off, and dredge each piece in the flour mixture until fully coated.

In a large skillet or deep fryer, heat about 1 inch of vegetable oil over medium-high heat until it reaches 350°F. Carefully add the chicken pieces in batches, being sure not to overcrowd the skillet. Fry the chicken for 12-15 minutes, turning occasionally, until golden brown and cooked through (internal temperature should reach 165°F).

Transfer the fried chicken to a paper towel-lined plate to drain excess oil. Serve hot and enjoy this crispy, juicy Southern classic with family and friends.

BBQ Ribs

Servings: 6

Ingredients:
- 3-4 lbs pork spare ribs or baby back ribs
- 1 tablespoon paprika
- 1 tablespoon garlic powder
- 1 teaspoon chili powder
- 1 teaspoon black pepper
- 1 teaspoon salt
- 1/2 cup apple cider vinegar
- 1 cup BBQ sauce (homemade or store-bought)

Nutritional Values (per serving):
- Calories: 680
- Fat: 45g
- Saturated Fat: 16g
- Cholesterol: 140mg
- Sodium: 900mg
- Carbohydrates: 18g
- Fiber: 2g
- Sugars: 12g
- Protein: 48g

Instructions:

Begin by preheating your oven to 300°F. In a small bowl, combine the paprika, garlic powder, chili powder, black pepper, and salt to create a dry rub. Rub the spice mixture generously over both sides of the ribs.

Place the ribs on a large piece of aluminum foil and drizzle the apple cider vinegar over the top. Wrap the ribs tightly in the foil and place them on a baking sheet. Bake in the oven for 2 1/2 to 3 hours, or until the ribs are tender and the meat easily pulls away from the bone.

Remove the ribs from the oven and unwrap them. Brush the ribs generously with BBQ sauce and either return them to the oven under the broiler for 5-7 minutes, or transfer them to a grill over medium heat for 5 minutes, allowing the sauce to caramelize and develop a sticky glaze.

Slice the ribs and serve with extra BBQ sauce on the side. These fall-off-the-bone ribs are perfect for a summer cookout or any family gathering.

Grilled Salmon With Dill

Servings: 4

Ingredients:

- 4 salmon fillets (about 6 oz each)
- 2 tablespoons olive oil
- 1 tablespoon fresh lemon juice
- 2 tablespoons fresh dill, chopped
- 2 garlic cloves, minced
- Salt and black pepper, to taste
- Lemon wedges, for serving

Nutritional Values (per serving):

- Calories: 360
- Fat: 24g
- Saturated Fat: 4g
- Cholesterol: 80mg
- Sodium: 180mg
- Carbohydrates: 2g
- Fiber: 0g
- Sugars: 0g
- Protein: 34g

Instructions:

Begin by preheating your grill to medium-high heat. In a small bowl, whisk together the olive oil, lemon juice, chopped dill, minced garlic, salt, and black pepper.

Brush both sides of the salmon fillets with the olive oil mixture. Place the salmon fillets skin-side down on the preheated grill and cook for 4-5 minutes per side, or until the salmon is opaque and flakes easily with a fork.

Remove the salmon from the grill and let it rest for a minute. Serve with lemon wedges and enjoy this light, flavorful dish that pairs perfectly with grilled vegetables or a fresh salad.

Shrimp And Grits

Servings: 4

Ingredients:
- 1 lb large shrimp, peeled and deveined
- 1 cup stone-ground grits
- 4 cups water
- 1 cup shredded cheddar cheese
- 4 slices bacon, chopped
- 1 small onion, diced
- 1 bell pepper, diced
- 2 garlic cloves, minced
- 1/4 cup chicken broth
- 2 tablespoons butter
- 1 tablespoon hot sauce (optional)
- Salt and black pepper, to taste
- Fresh parsley, chopped (for garnish)

Nutritional Values (per serving):
- Calories: 480
- Fat: 25g
- Saturated Fat: 12g
- Cholesterol: 220mg
- Sodium: 640mg
- Carbohydrates: 30g
- Fiber: 2g
- Sugars: 3g
- Protein: 32g

Instructions:

Start by bringing 4 cups of water to a boil in a medium saucepan. Stir in the stone-ground grits and reduce the heat to low. Cook, stirring frequently, for 20-25 minutes, or until the grits are thick and creamy. Stir in the butter, shredded cheddar cheese, and season with salt and pepper to taste. Set aside and keep warm.

In a large skillet, cook the chopped bacon over medium heat until crisp. Remove the bacon and set it aside, leaving about 2 tablespoons of bacon grease in the skillet. Add the diced onion, bell pepper, and garlic to the skillet and sauté for 3-4 minutes, until softened.

Add the shrimp to the skillet and cook for 2-3 minutes on each side, or until they turn pink being careful not to overcook them.. Stir in the chicken broth, butter, and hot sauce (if using), and cook for an additional 2-3 minutes until the sauce thickens slightly.

To serve, spoon the cheesy grits onto plates and top with the shrimp mixture. Sprinkle with the cooked bacon and fresh parsley. Enjoy this Southern classic, perfect for a comforting breakfast or dinner.

Roast Lamb With Mint Jelly

Servings: 6-8

Ingredients:
- 1 (4-5 lb) bone-in leg of lamb
- 4 garlic cloves, minced
- 2 tablespoons olive oil
- 1 tablespoon fresh rosemary, chopped (or 1 teaspoon dried)
- 1 tablespoon fresh thyme (or 1 teaspoon dried)
- Salt and black pepper, to taste
- 1/2 cup mint jelly (store-bought or homemade)

Nutritional Values (per serving):
- Calories: 480
- Fat: 30g
- Saturated Fat: 11g
- Cholesterol: 140mg
- Sodium: 240mg
- Carbohydrates: 6g
- Fiber: 0g
- Sugars: 4g
- Protein: 40g

Instructions:

Preheat your oven to 350°F. In a small bowl, combine the minced garlic, olive oil, chopped rosemary, thyme, salt, and black pepper to create a rub for the lamb.

Rub the garlic and herb mixture all over the leg of lamb, making sure it is evenly coated. Place the lamb on a rack in a roasting pan.

Roast the lamb for 1 1/2 to 2 hours, or until the internal temperature reaches 135°F for medium-rare or 145°F for medium. Baste the lamb every 30 minutes with the pan juices to keep it moist.

Once the lamb is cooked to your desired doneness, remove it from the oven and let it rest for 15-20 minutes before carving.

Serve the roasted lamb with mint jelly on the side. This classic combination of tender lamb and sweet mint jelly is perfect for a special family meal or holiday gathering.

Corned Beef And Cabbage

Servings: 6-8

Ingredients:

- 3-4 lbs corned beef brisket with spice packet
- 10 cups water
- 1 bay leaf
- 1 tablespoon black peppercorns
- 1 small head of cabbage, cut into wedges
- 4 large carrots, peeled and cut into chunks
- 6-8 small red potatoes, halved
- Mustard or horseradish, for serving (optional)

Nutritional Values (per serving):

- Calories: 450
- Fat: 25g
- Saturated Fat: 9g
- Cholesterol: 115mg
- Sodium: 1,850mg
- Carbohydrates: 28g
- Fiber: 6g
- Sugars: 5g
- Protein: 30g

Instructions:

Begin by placing the corned beef brisket in a large pot or Dutch oven. Cover with water, leaving 1-2 inches of water above the brisket. Add the spice packet, bay leaf, and peppercorns. Bring the water to a boil, then reduce the heat to low and cover. Simmer the brisket for 2 1/2 to 3 hours, or until the meat is tender and easily pulls apart with a fork.

After the corned beef has simmered, add the carrots and potatoes to the pot. Cook for 20-25 minutes, or until the vegetables are tender.

During the last 10 minutes of cooking, add the cabbage wedges to the pot and simmer until tender.

Remove the corned beef from the pot and let it rest for 10 minutes before slicing. Serve the corned beef with the vegetables and a side of mustard or horseradish if desired. This traditional dish is perfect for family dinners, especially on St. Patrick's Day.

CHAPTER 5

SAVORY SIDES

Creamy Mashed Potatoes

Servings: 4

Ingredients:

- 3 large russet potatoes, peeled and cut into chunks
- 1/3 cup whole milk
- 3 tablespoons unsalted butter
- 3 tablespoons sour cream
- Salt and black pepper, to taste
- Fresh parsley, chopped (optional, for garnish)

Nutritional Values (per serving):

- Calories: 250
- Fat: 12g
- Saturated Fat: 7g
- Cholesterol: 30mg
- Sodium: 130mg
- Carbohydrates: 33g
- Fiber: 4g
- Sugars: 2g
- Protein: 4g

Instructions:

Place the potato chunks in a large pot and cover with cold water. Add a pinch of salt and bring the water to a boil. Reduce the heat to a simmer and cook the potatoes for 15-20 minutes, or until they are tender and easily pierced with a fork.

Drain the potatoes and return them to the pot. Add the milk, butter, and sour cream, then mash the potatoes using a potato masher or electric mixer until smooth and creamy. Season with salt and black pepper to taste.

Transfer the mashed potatoes to a serving bowl and garnish with fresh parsley if desired. Serve warm and enjoy.

Green Beans Almondine

Servings: 4

Ingredients:

- 3/4 lb fresh green beans, trimmed
- 3 tablespoons sliced almonds
- 1 1/2 tablespoons unsalted butter
- 1 garlic clove, minced
- 1/2 tablespoon fresh lemon juice
- Salt and black pepper, to taste
- Fresh parsley, chopped (optional, for garnish)

Nutritional Values (per serving):

- Calories: 130
- Fat: 10g
- Saturated Fat: 4g
- Cholesterol: 10mg
- Sodium: 100mg
- Carbohydrates: 8g
- Fiber: 3g
- Sugars: 2g
- Protein: 3g

Instructions:

Begin by blanching the green beans in a large pot of salted boiling water for 3-4 minutes, until they are bright green and tender-crisp. Drain the beans and immediately transfer them to an ice water bath to stop the cooking process. Drain and set aside.

In a large skillet, melt the butter over medium heat. Add the sliced almonds and toast them for 2-3 minutes, stirring frequently, until they are golden brown. Add the minced garlic and cook for another minute until fragrant.

Add the blanched green beans to the skillet and toss to combine. Sauté for 2-3 minutes until the beans are heated through. Drizzle with fresh lemon juice and season with salt and black pepper to taste.

Transfer to a serving dish and garnish with chopped parsley if desired.

Caramelized Onion and Bacon Brussels Sprouts

Servings: 4

Ingredients:

- 1 lb Brussels sprouts, trimmed and halved
- 3 slices bacon, chopped
- 1 small onion, thinly sliced
- 1 1/2 tablespoons olive oil
- 2 teaspoons balsamic vinegar
- Salt and black pepper, to taste

Nutritional Values (per serving):

- Calories: 180
- Fat: 11g
- Saturated Fat: 3g
- Cholesterol: 15mg
- Sodium: 250mg
- Carbohydrates: 15g
- Fiber: 5g
- Sugars: 5g
- Protein: 5g

Instructions:

Start by cooking the chopped bacon in a large skillet over medium heat until crispy, about 5-7 minutes. Remove the bacon with a slotted spoon and set aside, leaving the bacon grease in the skillet.

Add the sliced onions to the skillet and cook over medium heat, stirring occasionally, for about 10-12 minutes until they are caramelized and golden brown.

Meanwhile, in a separate large skillet, heat the olive oil over medium-high heat. Add the Brussels sprouts, cut side down, and cook for 5-6 minutes, or until they are browned and crispy. Stir and continue cooking for another 3-4 minutes until tender.

Toss the caramelized onions and cooked bacon with the Brussels sprouts. Drizzle with balsamic vinegar and season with salt and black pepper to taste.

Serve this savory, flavorful side dish warm.

Glazed Carrots With Brown Sugar

Servings: 4

Ingredients:

- 1 lb carrots, peeled and sliced
- 2 tablespoons unsalted butter
- 2 tablespoons brown sugar
- 1 tablespoon honey
- 1/4 teaspoon ground cinnamon (optional)
- Salt and black pepper, to taste
- Fresh parsley, chopped (optional, for garnish)

Nutritional Values (per serving):

- Calories: 150
- Fat: 6g
- Saturated Fat: 3g
- Cholesterol: 15mg
- Sodium: 120mg
- Carbohydrates: 22g
- Fiber: 3g
- Sugars: 15g
- Protein: 2g

Instructions:

Begin by placing the sliced carrots in a large pot of boiling salted water. Cook for 5-7 minutes, or until the carrots are tender but not mushy. Drain the carrots and set them aside.

In a large skillet, melt the butter over medium heat. Stir in the brown sugar, honey, and cinnamon (if using), cooking until the sugar has dissolved and the mixture is smooth, about 2-3 minutes.

Add the cooked carrots to the skillet, tossing them to coat in the glaze. Cook for an additional 3-4 minutes, stirring occasionally, until the carrots are caramelized and coated in the sweet glaze.

Season with salt and black pepper to taste, and garnish with fresh parsley if desired. Serve warm as a delicious, sweet side dish.

Southern Collard Greens

Servings: 4

Ingredients:
- 1 lb fresh collard greens, washed and chopped
- 3 slices bacon, chopped
- 1/2 small onion, chopped
- 1 garlic clove, minced
- 3 cups chicken broth
- 2 teaspoons apple cider vinegar
- 1/4 teaspoon red pepper flakes (optional)
- Salt and black pepper, to taste

Nutritional Values (per serving):
- Calories: 180
- Fat: 10g
- Saturated Fat: 4g
- Cholesterol: 20mg
- Sodium: 520mg
- Carbohydrates: 10g
- Fiber: 4g
- Sugars: 1g
- Protein: 8g

Instructions:

Begin by cooking the chopped bacon in a large pot over medium heat until crispy, about 5-7 minutes. Remove the bacon with a slotted spoon and set it aside, leaving the bacon grease in the pot.

Add the chopped onion to the pot and cook for 3-4 minutes, or until softened. Stir in the minced garlic and cook for another minute until fragrant.

Add the chopped collard greens to the pot, stirring to coat them in the bacon grease. Pour in the chicken broth, apple cider vinegar, and red pepper flakes (if using). Bring the mixture to a boil, then reduce the heat to low, cover, and simmer for 45 minutes to 1 hour, or until the greens are tender.

Stir in the cooked bacon and season with salt and black pepper to taste. Serve these flavorful greens warm.

Cheddar And Chive Scones

Servings: 4

Ingredients:

- 1 1/2 cups all-purpose flour
- 1 1/2 teaspoons baking powder
- 1/4 teaspoon salt
- 1/4 teaspoon black pepper
- 1/4 cup unsalted butter, cold and cubed
- 3/4 cup shredded sharp cheddar cheese
- 2 tablespoons chopped fresh chives
- 1/2 cup buttermilk

Nutritional Values (per serving):

- Calories: 240
- Fat: 12g
- Saturated Fat: 7g
- Cholesterol: 40mg
- Sodium: 330mg
- Carbohydrates: 25g
- Fiber: 1g
- Sugars: 2g
- Protein: 7g

Instructions:

Preheat your oven to 400°F. In a large mixing bowl, whisk together the flour, baking powder, salt, and black pepper. Using a pastry cutter or your fingers, cut in the cold butter until the mixture resembles coarse crumbs.

Stir in the shredded cheddar cheese and chopped chives. Gradually add the buttermilk, stirring just until the dough comes together. Be careful not to overmix.

Turn the dough out onto a lightly floured surface and gently pat it into a 1-inch thick round. Cut the dough into 4 wedges and place them on a parchment-lined baking sheet.

Bake for 12-15 minutes, or until the scones are golden brown on the edges. Let them cool slightly before serving.

Sautéed Mushrooms

Servings: 4

Ingredients:

- 1 lb cremini or button mushrooms, cleaned and sliced
- 2 tablespoons unsalted butter
- 1 tablespoon olive oil
- 1 garlic clove, minced
- 1 teaspoon fresh thyme leaves (optional)
- Salt and black pepper, to taste
- Fresh parsley, chopped (optional, for garnish)

Nutritional Values (per serving):

- Calories: 120
- Fat: 9g
- Saturated Fat: 4g
- Cholesterol: 15mg
- Sodium: 60mg
- Carbohydrates: 7g
- Fiber: 2g
- Sugars: 3g
- Protein: 4g

Instructions:

In a large skillet, heat the butter and olive oil over medium-high heat. Add the sliced mushrooms in an even layer and cook for 4-5 minutes without stirring, allowing them to brown.

Once the mushrooms are browned on one side, stir them and continue cooking for another 3-4 minutes until they are golden and tender. Add the minced garlic and thyme, if using, and cook for an additional minute until fragrant.

Season with salt and black pepper to taste. Garnish with fresh parsley if desired.

Zucchini And Tomato Gratin

Servings: 4

Ingredients:

- 2 medium zucchini, sliced into 1/4-inch rounds
- 2 medium tomatoes, sliced into 1/4-inch rounds
- 1/3 cup grated Parmesan cheese
- 1/3 cup shredded mozzarella cheese
- 3 tablespoons breadcrumbs
- 1 1/2 tablespoons olive oil
- 1 garlic clove, minced
- 3/4 teaspoon dried Italian herbs (or fresh basil and oregano)
- Salt and black pepper, to taste

Nutritional Values (per serving):

- Calories: 160
- Fat: 11g
- Saturated Fat: 4g
- Cholesterol: 8mg
- Sodium: 220mg
- Carbohydrates: 8g
- Fiber: 2g
- Sugars: 4g
- Protein: 6g

Instructions:

Preheat your oven to 375°F. Lightly grease a baking dish. Arrange the zucchini and tomato slices in alternating rows, slightly overlapping each slice.

In a small bowl, mix together the Parmesan cheese, mozzarella cheese, breadcrumbs, olive oil, garlic, and Italian herbs. Season with salt and black pepper to taste.

Sprinkle the cheese and breadcrumb mixture evenly over the zucchini and tomatoes.

Bake for 20-25 minutes, or until the vegetables are tender and the topping is golden brown and crispy. Serve warm as a delicious side dish for any meal.

Roasted Asparagus

Servings: 4

Ingredients:

- 1 lb fresh asparagus, trimmed
- 1 1/2 tablespoons olive oil
- 1 garlic clove, minced
- Salt and black pepper, to taste
- 2 teaspoons fresh lemon juice (optional)
- Grated Parmesan cheese (optional, for garnish)

Nutritional Values (per serving):

- Calories: 85
- Fat: 7g
- Saturated Fat: 1g
- Cholesterol: 0mg
- Sodium: 8mg
- Carbohydrates: 5g
- Fiber: 2g
- Sugars: 2g
- Protein: 2g

Instructions:

Preheat your oven to 400°F. Spread the asparagus in a single layer on a baking sheet. Drizzle with olive oil and sprinkle with minced garlic, salt, and black pepper.

Roast the asparagus for 12-15 minutes, or until tender and lightly browned. For added flavor, drizzle with fresh lemon juice and sprinkle with grated Parmesan cheese before serving.

Serve this simple yet elegant side dish warm, and enjoy the fresh, bright flavors that complement any main course.

Garlic Butter Rice

Servings: 4

Ingredients:

- 1 1/2 cups long-grain white rice
- 2 1/4 cups chicken broth (or water)
- 3 tablespoons unsalted butter
- 3 garlic cloves, minced
- 1/2 teaspoon salt
- 1/4 teaspoon black pepper
- Fresh parsley, chopped (optional, for garnish)

Nutritional Values (per serving):

- Calories: 240
- Fat: 8g
- Saturated Fat: 5g
- Cholesterol: 20mg
- Sodium: 200mg
- Carbohydrates: 38g
- Fiber: 1g
- Sugars: 0g
- Protein: 3g

Instructions:

Begin by melting the butter in a medium saucepan over medium heat. Add the minced garlic and sauté for 1-2 minutes, until fragrant but not browned.

Add the rice to the saucepan, stirring to coat the grains in the garlic butter. Pour in the chicken broth and season with salt and black pepper.

Bring the mixture to a boil, then reduce the heat to low, cover, and simmer for 15-18 minutes, or until the rice is tender and the liquid is absorbed.

Remove the saucepan from heat and let the rice sit, covered, for 5 minutes. Fluff the rice with a fork and garnish with fresh parsley if desired. Serve this flavorful garlic butter rice alongside any main dish for a simple, yet delicious side.

Cauliflower Gratin

Servings: 4

Ingredients:

- 1 medium head of cauliflower, cut into florets
- 1 1/2 tablespoons unsalted butter
- 1 1/2 tablespoons all-purpose flour
- 1 1/4 cups whole milk
- 3/4 cup shredded Gruyère or cheddar cheese
- 3 tablespoons grated Parmesan cheese
- 1/3 cup breadcrumbs
- Salt and black pepper, to taste
- Fresh thyme (optional, for garnish)

Nutritional Values (per serving):

- Calories: 230
- Fat: 14g
- Saturated Fat: 8g
- Cholesterol: 35mg
- Sodium: 240mg
- Carbohydrates: 14g
- Fiber: 3g
- Sugars: 4g
- Protein: 10g

Instructions:

Preheat your oven to 375°F. Lightly grease a baking dish. Bring a large pot of salted water to a boil and blanch the cauliflower florets for 3-4 minutes, until tender but still firm. Drain and set aside.

In a medium saucepan, melt the butter over medium heat. Whisk in the flour and cook for 1-2 minutes to form a roux. Gradually whisk in the milk, stirring constantly until the mixture thickens, about 3-4 minutes.

Remove the saucepan from heat and stir in the shredded Gruyère or cheddar cheese. Season with salt and black pepper to taste.

Arrange the cauliflower florets in the prepared baking dish and pour the cheese sauce over the top, ensuring the cauliflower is well-coated. In a small bowl, mix the breadcrumbs with the grated Parmesan cheese and sprinkle the mixture over the cauliflower.

Bake for 20-25 minutes, or until the top is golden brown and bubbly. Garnish with fresh thyme if desired, and serve this creamy, cheesy cauliflower gratin as a delicious side dish.

CHAPTER 6

GARDEN-FRESH SALADS

Grandma's Potato Salad

Servings: 4

Ingredients:

- 1 1/2 lbs russet potatoes, peeled and cut into chunks
- 2 large eggs, hard-boiled and chopped
- 1/4 cup finely chopped onion
- 1/4 cup finely chopped celery
- 1/2 cup mayonnaise
- 1 tablespoon yellow mustard
- 1 tablespoon sweet pickle relish
- Salt and black pepper, to taste
- Paprika (optional, for garnish)

Nutritional Values (per serving):

- Calories: 290
- Fat: 18g
- Saturated Fat: 3g
- Cholesterol: 110mg
- Sodium: 310mg
- Carbohydrates: 29g
- Fiber: 3g
- Sugars: 4g
- Protein: 6g

Instructions:

Begin by placing the potato chunks in a large pot of salted water. Bring the water to a boil and cook the potatoes for 10-12 minutes, or until they are tender but not mushy. Drain and allow them to cool slightly.

In a large mixing bowl, combine the chopped eggs, onion, and celery. In a separate small bowl, whisk together the mayonnaise, mustard, pickle relish, salt, and black pepper.

Gently fold the potatoes into the egg and vegetable mixture. Pour the dressing over the potatoes and toss to coat evenly. Adjust the seasoning to taste.

Transfer the potato salad to a serving dish and sprinkle with paprika if desired. Chill in the refrigerator for at least 1 hour before serving. Enjoy this classic, comforting side dish at picnics, barbecues, or family dinners.

Sweet And Sour Coleslaw

Servings: 4

Ingredients:

- 1/2 small head of green cabbage, shredded
- 1 medium carrot, grated
- 1/4 small red onion, thinly sliced
- 1/4 cup apple cider vinegar
- 2 tablespoons sugar
- 1 tablespoon olive oil
- 1 teaspoon Dijon mustard
- Salt and black pepper, to taste

Nutritional Values (per serving):

- Calories: 100
- Fat: 4g
- Saturated Fat: 0.5g
- Cholesterol: 0mg
- Sodium: 90mg
- Carbohydrates: 14g
- Fiber: 3g
- Sugars: 10g
- Protein: 1g

Instructions:

In a large mixing bowl, combine the shredded cabbage, grated carrot, and thinly sliced red onion.

In a small bowl, whisk together the apple cider vinegar, sugar, olive oil, Dijon mustard, salt, and black pepper until the sugar has dissolved.

Pour the dressing over the cabbage mixture and toss to coat evenly. Let the coleslaw sit for at least 30 minutes to allow the flavors to meld together, stirring occasionally.

Serve chilled or at room temperature. This light, tangy coleslaw is a perfect complement to grilled meats or as a refreshing side dish for any meal.

Waldorf Salad As She Loved

Servings: 4

Ingredients:

- 2 medium apples, chopped (preferably a mix of sweet and tart varieties)
- 1/2 cup red seedless grapes, halved
- 1/2 cup chopped celery
- 1/4 cup chopped walnuts
- 1/4 cup mayonnaise
- 1 tablespoon lemon juice
- Salt and black pepper, to taste
- Fresh lettuce leaves, for serving

Nutritional Values (per serving):

- Calories: 210
- Fat: 14g
- Saturated Fat: 2g
- Cholesterol: 5mg
- Sodium: 150mg
- Carbohydrates: 24g
- Fiber: 4g
- Sugars: 18g
- Protein: 2g

Instructions:

In a large mixing bowl, toss together the chopped apples, grapes, celery, and walnuts.

In a small bowl, whisk together the mayonnaise, lemon juice, salt, and black pepper until smooth. Pour the dressing over the apple mixture and gently toss to combine.

Serve the Waldorf salad on a bed of fresh lettuce leaves. This classic and refreshing salad makes for a perfect side dish at brunches, luncheons, or holiday gatherings.

Spinach Salad With Hot Bacon Dressing

Servings: 4

Ingredients:

- 6 cups fresh spinach leaves, washed and dried
- 4 slices bacon, chopped
- 1/2 small red onion, thinly sliced
- 2 hard-boiled eggs, sliced
- 1/4 cup apple cider vinegar
- 1 tablespoon sugar
- 1 teaspoon Dijon mustard
- Salt and black pepper, to taste

Nutritional Values (per serving):

- Calories: 230
- Fat: 18g
- Saturated Fat: 5g
- Cholesterol: 150mg
- Sodium: 400mg
- Carbohydrates: 8g
- Fiber: 3g
- Sugars: 5g
- Protein: 10g

Instructions:

In a large skillet, cook the chopped bacon over medium heat until crispy, about 5-7 minutes. Remove the bacon with a slotted spoon and set aside, leaving the bacon grease in the skillet.

Add the sliced red onion to the skillet and sauté for 2-3 minutes, until softened. Stir in the apple cider vinegar, sugar, and Dijon mustard. Cook for another 2 minutes, stirring constantly until the dressing is well-combined. Season with salt and black pepper to taste.

In a large bowl, toss the fresh spinach leaves with the warm bacon dressing until evenly coated. Top the salad with the cooked bacon and sliced hard-boiled eggs.

Serve immediately and enjoy this warm, savory salad as a satisfying side or light main dish.

Caesar Salad

Servings: 4

Ingredients:

- 1 large head of romaine lettuce, chopped
- 1/2 cup Caesar dressing (store-bought or homemade)
- 1/4 cup grated Parmesan cheese
- 1 cup croutons
- 1 tablespoon lemon juice
- Freshly ground black pepper, to taste

Nutritional Values (per serving):

- Calories: 220
- Fat: 17g
- Saturated Fat: 3g
- Cholesterol: 10mg
- Sodium: 480mg
- Carbohydrates: 14g
- Fiber: 4g
- Sugars: 2g
- Protein: 6g

Instructions:

In a large mixing bowl, toss the chopped romaine lettuce with Caesar dressing until evenly coated. Add the grated Parmesan cheese and croutons, and gently toss again.

Drizzle the salad with fresh lemon juice and sprinkle with freshly ground black pepper to taste.

Serve this classic Caesar salad as a starter or side dish for any meal. Optionally, top with grilled chicken or shrimp for a heartier version.

Greek Village Salad

Servings: 4

Ingredients:
- 2 medium tomatoes, chopped
- 1 cucumber, peeled and sliced
- 1/2 red onion, thinly sliced
- 1/4 cup Kalamata olives, pitted
- 1/4 cup feta cheese, crumbled
- 2 tablespoons extra-virgin olive oil
- 1 tablespoon red wine vinegar
- 1 teaspoon dried oregano
- Salt and black pepper, to taste

Nutritional Values (per serving):
- Calories: 180
- Fat: 15g
- Saturated Fat: 4g
- Cholesterol: 15mg
- Sodium: 280mg
- Carbohydrates: 9g
- Fiber: 2g
- Sugars: 5g
- Protein: 4g

Instructions:

In a large mixing bowl, combine the chopped tomatoes, cucumber slices, red onion, and Kalamata olives.

Drizzle with olive oil and red wine vinegar, then sprinkle with dried oregano. Season with salt and black pepper to taste.

Gently toss the salad to combine, then top with crumbled feta cheese. Serve chilled or at room temperature as a refreshing side dish for any Mediterranean-inspired meal.

Cobb Salad

Servings: 4

Ingredients:

- 4 cups chopped romaine or mixed greens
- 1 cooked chicken breast, diced
- 2 hard-boiled eggs, chopped
- 1/2 avocado, sliced
- 1/2 cup cherry tomatoes, halved
- 1/4 cup crumbled blue cheese
- 2 slices bacon, cooked and crumbled
- 2 tablespoons red wine vinegar
- 3 tablespoons olive oil
- 1 teaspoon Dijon mustard
- Salt and black pepper, to taste

Nutritional Values (per serving):

- Calories: 400
- Fat: 28g
- Saturated Fat: 7g
- Cholesterol: 180mg
- Sodium: 430mg
- Carbohydrates: 8g
- Fiber: 4g
- Sugars: 2g
- Protein: 25g

Instructions:

Arrange the chopped greens on a large serving platter. Top with diced chicken, hard-boiled eggs, avocado slices, cherry tomatoes, crumbled blue cheese, and crumbled bacon.

In a small bowl, whisk together the red wine vinegar, olive oil, Dijon mustard, salt, and black pepper to create a vinaigrette.

Drizzle the vinaigrette over the salad, toss gently if desired, and serve immediately. This hearty and flavorful salad can serve as a satisfying main dish or a fresh side.

CHAPTER 7

BELOVED BREADS & ROLLS

Skillet Cornbread

Servings: 4

Ingredients:

- 1 cup yellow cornmeal
- 1/2 cup all-purpose flour
- 2 tablespoons sugar
- 1 teaspoon baking powder
- 1/2 teaspoon baking soda
- 1/4 teaspoon salt
- 1 cup buttermilk
- 1 large egg
- 2 tablespoons unsalted butter, melted
- 1 tablespoon vegetable oil (for the skillet)

Nutritional Values (per serving):

- Calories: 210
- Fat: 10g
- Saturated Fat: 4g
- Cholesterol: 55mg
- Sodium: 240mg
- Carbohydrates: 27g
- Fiber: 2g
- Sugars: 6g
- Protein: 5g

Instructions:

Preheat your oven to 400°F. Heat a cast-iron skillet over medium heat and add the vegetable oil to coat the bottom. Once hot, place the skillet in the oven to heat while you prepare the batter.

In a large bowl, whisk together the cornmeal, flour, sugar, baking powder, baking soda, and salt. In a separate bowl, whisk together the buttermilk, egg, and melted butter. Stir the wet ingredients into the dry ingredients until just combined.

Carefully remove the hot skillet from the oven and pour in the cornbread batter, spreading it evenly. Return the skillet to the oven and bake for 15-20 minutes, or until the top is golden brown and a toothpick inserted in the center comes out clean.

Serve the cornbread warm, and enjoy this Southern classic with butter, honey, or as a side to chili or soup.

Sunday Dinner Rolls

Servings: 4

Ingredients:

- 1/2 packet active dry yeast (about 1 1/4 teaspoons)
- 1/4 cup warm water (110°F)
- 1 tablespoon sugar
- 1 1/4 cups all-purpose flour
- 1/4 teaspoon salt
- 2 tablespoons unsalted butter, softened
- 1/4 cup milk, warmed
- 1 large egg
- 1 tablespoon melted butter (for brushing)

Nutritional Values (per serving):

- Calories: 220
- Fat: 10g
- Saturated Fat: 5g
- Cholesterol: 70mg
- Sodium: 150mg
- Carbohydrates: 25g
- Fiber: 1g
- Sugars: 5g
- Protein: 5g

Instructions:

In a small bowl, dissolve the yeast and sugar in warm water and let sit for 5-10 minutes until frothy.

In a large bowl, mix the flour and salt. Add the softened butter, milk, egg, and yeast mixture. Stir until a soft dough forms. Turn the dough out onto a floured surface and knead for 5-7 minutes, until smooth and elastic.

Place the dough in a greased bowl, cover, and let rise in a warm place for 1 hour, or until doubled in size.

Punch down the dough and divide into 8 equal portions. Shape each portion into a ball and place on a greased baking sheet. Let the rolls rise for another 20-30 minutes.

Preheat the oven to 375°F. Brush the rolls with melted butter and bake for 12-15 minutes, or until golden brown. Brush with more butter after baking, and serve warm with your favorite meal.

Grandma's Garlic Knots

Servings: 4

Ingredients:

- 1/2 packet active dry yeast (about 1 1/4 teaspoons)
- 1/4 cup warm water (110°F)
- 1 1/4 cups all-purpose flour
- 1/4 teaspoon salt
- 1 tablespoon olive oil
- 1/4 cup warm milk
- 1 garlic clove, minced
- 2 tablespoons melted butter
- 1 tablespoon chopped fresh parsley
- 1/4 teaspoon garlic powder
- Salt, to taste

Nutritional Values (per serving):

- Calories: 190
- Fat: 8g
- Saturated Fat: 3g
- Cholesterol: 15mg
- Sodium: 220mg
- Carbohydrates: 25g
- Fiber: 1g
- Sugars: 2g
- Protein: 5g

Instructions:

In a small bowl, dissolve the yeast in warm water and let it sit for 5-10 minutes until frothy.

In a large bowl, combine the flour and salt. Add the olive oil, warm milk, and yeast mixture. Stir until the dough comes together. Knead the dough on a floured surface for 5-7 minutes until smooth.

Place the dough in a greased bowl, cover, and let it rise in a warm place for 1 hour, or until doubled in size.

Punch down the dough and divide it into 8 equal pieces. Roll each piece into a rope and tie into a knot. Place the knots on a greased baking sheet and let them rise for another 20-30 minutes.

Preheat the oven to 375°F. Mix the melted butter, minced garlic, parsley, garlic powder, and salt in a small bowl. Brush the garlic butter over the knots.

Bake for 12-15 minutes, or until golden brown. Brush with more garlic butter after baking, and enjoy these delicious, fragrant garlic knots with pasta or soups.

Whole Wheat Honey Bread

Servings: 4

Ingredients:

- 1/2 packet active dry yeast (about 1 1/4 teaspoons)
- 1/4 cup warm water (110°F)
- 1 tablespoon honey
- 3/4 cup whole wheat flour
- 1/2 cup all-purpose flour
- 1/4 teaspoon salt
- 1 tablespoon olive oil
- 1/4 cup warm milk

Nutritional Values (per serving):

- Calories: 180
- Fat: 6g
- Saturated Fat: 1g
- Cholesterol: 0mg
- Sodium: 130mg
- Carbohydrates: 29g
- Fiber: 3g
- Sugars: 5g
- Protein: 5g

Instructions:

In a small bowl, dissolve the yeast and honey in warm water and let sit for 5-10 minutes until frothy.

In a large mixing bowl, combine the whole wheat flour, all-purpose flour, and salt. Add the olive oil, warm milk, and yeast mixture. Stir until a soft dough forms. Knead the dough on a floured surface for 5-7 minutes until smooth and elastic.

Place the dough in a greased bowl, cover, and let it rise in a warm place for 1 hour, or until doubled in size.

Punch down the dough and shape it into a small loaf. Place the loaf in a greased 8x4-inch loaf pan and let it rise for another 30 minutes.

Preheat your oven to 350°F. Bake the bread for 20-25 minutes, or until golden brown and sounds hollow when tapped on the bottom.

Let cool before slicing. This slightly sweet, hearty whole wheat bread is perfect for sandwiches or to serve alongside butter and jam.

Pumpkin Scones

Servings: 4

Ingredients:

- 1 cup all-purpose flour
- 1 tablespoon sugar
- 1 teaspoon baking powder
- 1/2 teaspoon ground cinnamon
- 1/4 teaspoon ground nutmeg
- 1/4 teaspoon ground ginger
- 1/4 teaspoon salt
- 2 tablespoons cold unsalted butter, cubed
- 1/4 cup pumpkin puree
- 2 tablespoons milk
- 1/2 teaspoon vanilla extract
- 1/4 cup powdered sugar (for glaze)
- 1 tablespoon milk (for glaze)

Nutritional Values (per serving):

- Calories: 180
- Fat: 8g
- Saturated Fat: 5g
- Cholesterol: 15mg
- Sodium: 150mg
- Carbohydrates: 25g
- Fiber: 2g
- Sugars: 8g
- Protein: 3g

Instructions:

Preheat your oven to 400°F. Line a baking sheet with parchment paper.

In a large bowl, whisk together the flour, sugar, baking powder, cinnamon, nutmeg, ginger, and salt. Using a pastry cutter or your fingers, cut the cold butter into the dry ingredients until the mixture resembles coarse crumbs.

In a separate bowl, whisk together the pumpkin puree, milk, and vanilla extract. Gradually add the wet ingredients to the dry ingredients, mixing just until combined.

Turn the dough out onto a lightly floured surface and shape it into a small round, about 1-inch thick. Cut the dough into 4 wedges and place them on the prepared baking sheet.

Bake for 12-15 minutes, or until the scones are golden brown. Allow them to cool slightly before drizzling with a glaze made from powdered sugar and milk. Enjoy these cozy, spiced scones with a warm drink.

Banana Nut Bread

Servings: 4

Ingredients:

- 1/2 cup mashed ripe bananas (about 1 large banana)
- 1/4 cup sugar
- 2 tablespoons unsalted butter, melted
- 1 large egg
- 1/2 teaspoon vanilla extract
- 3/4 cup all-purpose flour
- 1/4 teaspoon baking soda
- 1/4 teaspoon salt
- 1/4 cup chopped walnuts (optional)

Nutritional Values (per serving):

- Calories: 220
- Fat: 10g
- Saturated Fat: 5g
- Cholesterol: 45mg
- Sodium: 160mg
- Carbohydrates: 30g
- Fiber: 2g
- Sugars: 14g
- Protein: 4g

Instructions:

Preheat your oven to 350°F. Grease a small 8x4-inch loaf pan.

In a medium bowl, mix together the mashed banana, sugar, melted butter, egg, and vanilla extract until smooth.

In a separate bowl, whisk together the flour, baking soda, and salt. Gradually add the dry ingredients to the wet ingredients, stirring just until combined. Fold in the chopped walnuts, if using.

Pour the batter into the prepared loaf pan and smooth the top. Bake for 25-30 minutes, or until a toothpick inserted into the center comes out clean.

Let the banana nut bread cool in the pan for 10 minutes before transferring it to a wire rack to cool completely. Slice and enjoy this moist, flavorful bread for breakfast or a snack.

Buttermilk Biscuits

Servings: 4

Ingredients:

- 1 cup all-purpose flour
- 1 teaspoon baking powder
- 1/4 teaspoon baking soda
- 1/4 teaspoon salt
- 2 tablespoons unsalted butter, cold and cubed
- 1/2 cup buttermilk, cold

Nutritional Values (per serving):

- Calories: 180
- Fat: 8g
- Saturated Fat: 5g
- Cholesterol: 20mg
- Sodium: 210mg
- Carbohydrates: 22g
- Fiber: 1g
- Sugars: 1g
- Protein: 4g

Instructions:

Preheat your oven to 450°F and line a baking sheet with parchment paper.

In a large bowl, whisk together the flour, baking powder, baking soda, and salt. Using a pastry cutter or your fingers, cut in the cold butter until the mixture resembles coarse crumbs.

Add the cold buttermilk and stir until the dough comes together. Be careful not to overmix.

Turn the dough out onto a lightly floured surface and gently pat it into a 1-inch thick rectangle. Use a biscuit cutter to cut out 4 biscuits and place them on the prepared baking sheet.

Bake for 10-12 minutes, or until the biscuits are golden brown. Serve warm with butter or jam for a delicious addition to breakfast or dinner.

Angel Biscuits

Servings: 4

Ingredients:

- 1/2 packet active dry yeast (about 1 1/4 teaspoons)
- 1/4 cup warm water (110°F)
- 1 1/2 cups all-purpose flour
- 1 teaspoon baking powder
- 1/4 teaspoon baking soda
- 1/4 teaspoon salt
- 2 tablespoons sugar
- 1/4 cup unsalted butter, cold and cubed
- 1/2 cup buttermilk, cold

Nutritional Values (per serving):

- Calories: 220
- Fat: 10g
- Saturated Fat: 6g
- Cholesterol: 20mg
- Sodium: 240mg
- Carbohydrates: 28g
- Fiber: 1g
- Sugars: 5g
- Protein: 4g

Instructions:

In a small bowl, dissolve the yeast in warm water and let it sit for 5-10 minutes until frothy.

In a large bowl, whisk together the flour, baking powder, baking soda, salt, and sugar. Cut in the cold butter until the mixture resembles coarse crumbs.

Add the yeast mixture and cold buttermilk to the flour mixture, stirring until a soft dough forms.

Turn the dough out onto a lightly floured surface and knead gently for 1-2 minutes. Roll the dough out to 1/2-inch thickness and cut out 4 biscuits using a biscuit cutter.

Place the biscuits on a greased baking sheet and let them rise for 15 minutes. Preheat your oven to 425°F.

Bake the biscuits for 12-15 minutes, or until golden brown. Serve these light, fluffy biscuits warm with butter or honey.

CHAPTER 8

SWEET TREATS AND MEMORY MAKERS

Old-Fashioned Apple Pie

Servings: 4

Ingredients:

- 2 medium apples, peeled, cored, and thinly sliced
- 1/4 cup granulated sugar
- 1/4 cup brown sugar
- 1/2 teaspoon ground cinnamon
- 1/4 teaspoon ground nutmeg
- 1 tablespoon all-purpose flour
- 1/2 tablespoon lemon juice
- 1 prepared pie crust (store-bought or homemade)

Nutritional Values (per serving):

- Calories: 280
- Fat: 12g
- Saturated Fat: 5g
- Cholesterol: 10mg
- Sodium: 180mg
- Carbohydrates: 42g
- Fiber: 4g
- Sugars: 24g
- Protein: 2g

Instructions:

Preheat your oven to 375°F.

In a large bowl, combine the sliced apples, granulated sugar, brown sugar, cinnamon, nutmeg, flour, and lemon juice. Toss until the apples are evenly coated.

Roll out the pie crust and fit it into a 6-inch pie dish. Pour the apple mixture into the pie crust and spread it out evenly. Roll out a second pie crust (optional) and place it over the top, crimping the edges to seal. Cut a few small slits in the top for ventilation.

Bake for 35-40 minutes, or until the crust is golden brown and the filling is bubbly. Let the pie cool slightly before serving.

Serve warm with a scoop of vanilla ice cream for a classic treat.

Cherry Cobbler Like She Made

Servings: 4

Ingredients:
- 1 1/2 cups fresh or frozen cherries, pitted
- 1/4 cup granulated sugar
- 1 tablespoon cornstarch
- 1/4 cup water
- 1/2 teaspoon vanilla extract
- 1/2 cup all-purpose flour
- 1/4 cup sugar
- 1/2 teaspoon baking powder
- 1/8 teaspoon salt
- 2 tablespoons unsalted butter, melted
- 1/4 cup milk

Nutritional Values (per serving):
- Calories: 290
- Fat: 10g
- Saturated Fat: 6g
- Cholesterol: 30mg
- Sodium: 170mg
- Carbohydrates: 45g
- Fiber: 2g
- Sugars: 30g
- Protein: 3g

Instructions:

Preheat your oven to 350°F.

In a medium saucepan, combine the cherries, sugar, cornstarch, water, and vanilla extract. Cook over medium heat, stirring occasionally, until the mixture thickens and becomes bubbly, about 5-7 minutes. Remove from heat and set aside.

In a separate bowl, whisk together the flour, sugar, baking powder, and salt. Stir in the melted butter and milk until a smooth batter forms.

Pour the cherry mixture into a small greased baking dish. Drop spoonfuls of the batter over the cherries, spreading it out slightly.

Bake for 25-30 minutes, or until the top is golden brown and the filling is bubbling. Let cool slightly before serving.

Serve warm with a scoop of vanilla ice cream or whipped cream.

Chocolate Fudge Brownies

Servings: 4

Ingredients:

- 1/4 cup unsalted butter, melted
- 1/2 cup granulated sugar
- 1 large egg
- 1/2 teaspoon vanilla extract
- 1/4 cup all-purpose flour
- 1/4 cup cocoa powder
- 1/4 teaspoon baking powder
- 1/8 teaspoon salt
- 1/4 cup chocolate chips (optional)

Nutritional Values (per serving):

- Calories: 250
- Fat: 12g
- Saturated Fat: 7g
- Cholesterol: 70mg
- Sodium: 110mg
- Carbohydrates: 36g
- Fiber: 2g
- Sugars: 24g
- Protein: 4g

Instructions:

Preheat your oven to 350°F. Grease a small 8x4-inch baking dish or line it with parchment paper.

In a medium bowl, whisk together the melted butter and sugar. Add the egg and vanilla extract, and mix until smooth.

In a separate bowl, whisk together the flour, cocoa powder, baking powder, and salt. Gradually stir the dry ingredients into the wet ingredients until just combined. Fold in the chocolate chips, if using.

Pour the batter into the prepared baking dish and spread it out evenly. Bake for 18-22 minutes, or until a toothpick inserted into the center comes out with a few moist crumbs.

Let the brownies cool before cutting them into squares. Serve as a decadent dessert or snack.

Classic Carrot Cake With Cream Cheese Frosting

Servings: 4

Ingredients:

For the cake:

- 1/2 cup all-purpose flour
- 1/2 teaspoon baking powder
- 1/4 teaspoon baking soda
- 1/2 teaspoon ground cinnamon
- 1/8 teaspoon ground nutmeg
- 1/8 teaspoon salt
- 1/2 cup grated carrots
- 1/4 cup vegetable oil
- 1/4 cup granulated sugar
- 1 large egg
- 1/2 teaspoon vanilla extract

For the frosting:

- 2 oz cream cheese, softened
- 1 tablespoon unsalted butter, softened
- 1/2 cup powdered sugar
- 1/2 teaspoon vanilla extract

Nutritional Values (per serving):

- Calories: 350
- Fat: 18g
- Saturated Fat: 7g
- Cholesterol: 55mg
- Sodium: 200mg
- Carbohydrates: 42g
- Fiber: 1g
- Sugars: 28g
- Protein: 4g

Instructions:

Preheat your oven to 350°F. Grease a small 6-inch round cake pan.

In a medium bowl, whisk together the flour, baking powder, baking soda, cinnamon, nutmeg, and salt.

In a separate bowl, whisk together the vegetable oil, sugar, egg, and vanilla extract. Stir in the grated carrots. Gradually add the dry ingredients to the wet ingredients, mixing until just combined. Pour the batter into the prepared cake pan and bake for 20-25 minutes, or until a toothpick inserted into the center comes out clean. Let the cake cool completely before frosting.

For the frosting: In a small bowl, beat together the softened cream cheese, butter, powdered sugar, and vanilla extract until smooth and creamy. Spread the frosting evenly over the cooled cake. Enjoy this classic, moist carrot cake!

Strawberry Rhubarb Crisp

Servings: 4

Ingredients:

For the filling:

- 1 cup chopped rhubarb
- 1 cup chopped strawberries
- 2 tablespoons granulated sugar
- 1 tablespoon cornstarch
- 1/2 teaspoon lemon juice

For the topping:

- 1/4 cup all-purpose flour
- 1/4 cup rolled oats
- 2 tablespoons brown sugar
- 2 tablespoons unsalted butter, cold and cubed
- 1/4 teaspoon ground cinnamon

Nutritional Values (per serving):

- Calories: 240
- Fat: 10g
- Saturated Fat: 6g
- Cholesterol: 25mg
- Sodium: 40mg
- Carbohydrates: 38g
- Fiber: 4g
- Sugars: 20g
- Protein: 2g

Instructions:

Preheat your oven to 350°F. Grease a small 6-inch baking dish.

In a medium bowl, combine the chopped rhubarb, strawberries, granulated sugar, cornstarch, and lemon juice. Mix well and pour the filling into the prepared baking dish.

In another bowl, mix together the flour, rolled oats, brown sugar, and cinnamon. Cut in the cold butter with a pastry cutter or your fingers until the mixture resembles coarse crumbs. Sprinkle the topping evenly over the fruit mixture.

Bake for 25-30 minutes, or until the topping is golden brown and the filling is bubbly. Let the crisp cool slightly before serving.

Serve warm with a scoop of vanilla ice cream or whipped cream for a delightful treat.

Homemade Vanilla Ice Cream

Servings: 4

Ingredients:

- 1 cup heavy cream
- 1/2 cup whole milk
- 1/4 cup granulated sugar
- 1/2 teaspoon vanilla extract
- Pinch of salt

Nutritional Values (per serving):

- Calories: 250
- Fat: 20g
- Saturated Fat: 12g
- Cholesterol: 70mg
- Sodium: 40mg
- Carbohydrates: 17g
- Sugars: 16g
- Protein: 2g

Instructions:

In a medium mixing bowl, whisk together the heavy cream, whole milk, sugar, vanilla extract, and salt until the sugar is dissolved.

Pour the mixture into an ice cream maker and churn according to the manufacturer's instructions, usually 15-20 minutes.

Once the ice cream has reached a soft-serve consistency, transfer it to a freezer-safe container and freeze for at least 2 hours, or until firm.

Scoop and enjoy this rich and creamy homemade vanilla ice cream with your favorite toppings or alongside a warm dessert.

Peach Cobbler

Servings: 4

Ingredients:

For the filling:
- 2 medium peaches, peeled and sliced
- 2 tablespoons granulated sugar
- 1 teaspoon lemon juice
- 1/2 teaspoon vanilla extract

For the topping:
- 1/4 cup all-purpose flour
- 1/4 cup sugar
- 1/4 teaspoon baking powder
- 1/8 teaspoon salt
- 2 tablespoons unsalted butter, melted
- 2 tablespoons milk

Nutritional Values (per serving):
- Calories: 280
- Fat: 12g
- Saturated Fat: 7g
- Cholesterol: 35mg
- Sodium: 130mg
- Carbohydrates: 40g
- Fiber: 2g
- Sugars: 28g
- Protein: 3g

Instructions:

Preheat your oven to 350°F. Grease a small 6-inch baking dish.

In a medium bowl, toss the sliced peaches with sugar, lemon juice, and vanilla extract. Spread the peach mixture evenly in the prepared baking dish.

In another bowl, mix together the flour, sugar, baking powder, and salt. Stir in the melted butter and milk until a batter forms. Drop spoonfuls of the batter over the peaches, spreading it slightly.

Bake for 25-30 minutes, or until the topping is golden brown and the filling is bubbly. Let the cobbler cool slightly before serving.

Serve warm with a scoop of vanilla ice cream for a classic summer dessert.

Blackberry Pie

Servings: 4

Ingredients:

- 1 1/2 cups fresh or frozen blackberries
- 1/4 cup granulated sugar
- 1 tablespoon cornstarch
- 1/2 tablespoon lemon juice
- 1/2 teaspoon vanilla extract
- 1 prepared pie crust (6-inch, store-bought or homemade)
- 1 tablespoon butter, cut into small pieces (optional)

Nutritional Values (per serving):

- Calories: 260
- Fat: 12g
- Saturated Fat: 6g
- Cholesterol: 20mg
- Sodium: 180mg
- Carbohydrates: 36g
- Fiber: 5g
- Sugars: 20g
- Protein: 3g

Instructions:

Preheat your oven to 375°F.

In a medium bowl, gently toss the blackberries with sugar, cornstarch, lemon juice, and vanilla extract. Let the mixture sit for about 10 minutes to allow the flavors to meld.

Roll out the pie crust and fit it into a 6-inch pie dish. Pour the blackberry filling into the pie crust and dot the filling with butter, if using. Roll out another crust (optional) and place it on top, crimping the edges to seal. Cut a few small slits in the top to allow steam to escape.

Bake for 30-35 minutes, or until the crust is golden brown and the filling is bubbly. Let the pie cool slightly before serving.

Serve warm or at room temperature, with a dollop of whipped cream or a scoop of vanilla ice cream.

Red Velvet Cake

Servings: 4

Ingredients:

For the cake:

- 1/2 cup all-purpose flour
- 1/4 teaspoon baking soda
- 1/2 tablespoon cocoa powder
- 1/4 cup granulated sugar
- 2 tablespoons unsalted butter, softened
- 1 large egg
- 1/4 teaspoon vanilla extract
- 1/4 cup buttermilk
- 1/2 teaspoon white vinegar
- 1/2 teaspoon red food coloring

For the frosting:

- 2 oz cream cheese, softened
- 2 tablespoons unsalted butter, softened
- 1/2 cup powdered sugar
- 1/4 teaspoon vanilla extract

Nutritional Values (per serving):

- Calories: 340
- Fat: 18g
- Saturated Fat: 11g
- Cholesterol: 80mg
- Sodium: 170mg
- Carbohydrates: 42g
- Fiber: 1g
- Sugars: 30g
- Protein: 5g

Instructions:

Preheat your oven to 350°F. Grease a 6-inch round cake pan.

In a medium bowl, whisk together the flour, baking soda, and cocoa powder. In a separate bowl, cream together the softened butter and sugar until light and fluffy. Add the egg and vanilla extract, and beat until combined.

In another small bowl, mix the buttermilk, vinegar, and red food coloring. Gradually add the dry ingredients to the wet ingredients, alternating with the buttermilk mixture, and stir until just combined. Pour the batter into the prepared cake pan and bake for 20-25 minutes, or until a toothpick inserted into the center comes out clean. Allow the cake to cool completely before frosting.

For the frosting: In a small bowl, beat together the softened cream cheese, butter, powdered sugar, and vanilla extract until smooth and creamy. Frost the cooled cake and enjoy this vibrant, classic dessert.

Apple Cider Doughnuts

Servings: 4

Ingredients:
- 1/2 cup apple cider
- 1/4 cup granulated sugar
- 1 tablespoon brown sugar
- 1/4 teaspoon ground cinnamon
- 1/8 teaspoon ground nutmeg
- 1/2 cup all-purpose flour
- 1/4 teaspoon baking powder
- 1/8 teaspoon baking soda
- 1/4 teaspoon salt
- 1/4 cup buttermilk
- 1/2 large egg, lightly beaten
- 1/2 teaspoon vanilla extract
- 2 tablespoons unsalted butter, melted

Nutritional Values (per serving):
- Calories: 250
- Fat: 10g
- Saturated Fat: 6g
- Cholesterol: 35mg
- Sodium: 150mg
- Carbohydrates: 37g
- Fiber: 1g
- Sugars: 22g
- Protein: 3g

For the topping:
- 1/4 cup granulated sugar
- 1/2 teaspoon ground cinnamon
- 1 tablespoon melted butter

Instructions:

In a small saucepan, bring the apple cider to a boil and reduce it to about half its original volume (approximately 1/4 cup). Set aside to cool. In a medium bowl, whisk together the granulated sugar, brown sugar, cinnamon, nutmeg, flour, baking powder, baking soda, and salt. In a separate bowl, combine the reduced apple cider, buttermilk, egg, vanilla extract, and melted butter. Stir the wet ingredients into the dry ingredients until just combined.

Preheat your oven to 350°F and grease a mini doughnut pan. Spoon the batter into the doughnut molds, filling each about 2/3 full. Bake for 10-12 minutes, or until the doughnuts are golden brown and spring back when lightly pressed. Let them cool in the pan for 5 minutes before transferring to a wire rack.

For the topping: Mix together the sugar and cinnamon in a small bowl. Brush the warm doughnuts with melted butter, then dip them into the cinnamon sugar mixture to coat. Enjoy these sweet, spiced doughnuts with a cup of hot apple cider!

CHAPTER 9
Exclusive Bonuses

As a thank you for purchasing my book and for the trust you've placed in me, I wanted to give you a special gift of exclusive bonuses to enhance your journey through Grandma's kitchen.

To access them, simply scan the QR code below or visit the link: https://drive.google.com/drive/folders/1CnqSJJFxXCV1iXdWZ4Xllb2ObjZ8ys30?usp=sharing.

CHAPTER 10
Cooking Conversions

Volume Equivalents (Liquid)

US Standard	US Standard (oz.)	Metric (approximate)
2 tbsps.	1 fl. oz.	30 milliliter
¼ cup	2 fl. oz.	60 milliliter
½ cup	4 fl. oz.	120 milliliter
1 cup	8 fl. oz.	240 milliliter
1½ cups	12 fl. oz.	355 milliliter
2 cups or 1 pint	16 fl. oz.	475 milliliter
4 cups or 1 quart	32 fl. oz.	1 Liter
1 gallon	128 fl. oz.	4 Liter

Volume Equivalents (Dry)

US Standard	Metric (approximate)
⅛ tsp.	0.5 milliliter
¼ tsp.	1 milliliter
½ tsp.	2 milliliter
¾ tsp.	4 milliliter
1 tsp.	5 milliliter
1 tbsp.	15 milliliter
¼ cup	59 milliliter
⅓ cup	79 milliliter
½ cup	118 milliliter
⅔ cup	156 milliliter
¾ cup	177 milliliter

1 cup	235 milliliter
2 cups or 1 pint	475 milliliter
3 cups	700 milliliter
4 cups or 1 quart	1 Liter

Oven Temperatures

Fahrenheit (F)	Celsius (C) (approximate)
250 deg.F	120 °C
300 deg.F	150 °C
325 deg.F	160 °C
350 deg.F	180 °C
375 deg.F	190 °C
400 deg.F	200 °C
425 deg.F	220 °C
450 deg.F	230 °C

Weight Equivalents

US Standard	Metric (approximate)
1 tbsp.	15 g
½ oz.	15 g
1 oz.	30 g
2 oz.	60 g
4 oz.	115 g
8 oz.	225 g
12 oz.	340 g
16 oz. or 1 lb.	455 g

CONCLUSION

As we come to the close of this heartfelt culinary journey, I hope these recipes have not only filled your tables but also warmed your hearts. Each page of this cookbook carries the essence of a family tradition, meant to be savored and shared with those you love. Remember, these dishes are more than just meals; they are invitations to gather, to laugh, and to create memories that will last a lifetime.

In your kitchen, armed with a trusty apron and the right tools—a sharp set of knives, a sturdy mixer, and dependable pots and pans—you've embraced the art of cooking with joy and confidence. As you continue to explore these recipes, keep experimenting with flavors and textures, making each dish uniquely yours.

Cooking is a beautiful blend of art and science, seasoned with love. So whether you're whipping up a quick weekday dinner or preparing a feast for a holiday gathering, pour your heart into every step, from the first chop to the last sprinkle.

Thank you for bringing my recipes into your home. May your kitchen always be a place of warmth and happiness, where every meal is a celebration and every bite tells a story. Here's to delicious dishes, joyful gatherings, and the enduring magic of Grandma's kitchen. Happy cooking, dear ones!

Thank you for exploring this book with me. I have poured my heart into ensuring it meets high standards of insight and quality. Your feedback on Amazon would greatly aid in spreading the word and engaging others who share our interests. I am truly thankful for your support and any insights you can offer.

Warmly,

Helen Baker

Made in the USA
Monee, IL
16 February 2025